And Your Deserts
Shall Flower

By the same author:

PARABLE OF COMMUNITY
Basic Texts of Taizé

LIVING TODAY FOR GOD
DYNAMIC OF THE PROVISIONAL
VIOLENT FOR PEACE

Brother Roger's journal:
FESTIVAL WITHOUT END
STRUGGLE AND CONTEMPLATION
A LIFE WE NEVER DARED HOPE FOR
THE WONDER OF A LOVE

And Your Deserts Shall Flower

Shall Flower

(Fleurissent les déserts du coeur)

Journal 1977–1979

BROTHER ROGER OF TAIZÉ

MOWBRAY
LONDON & OXFORD

Copyright © les Presses de Taizé 1983

ISBN 0 264 66990 8

First published in English 1984
by A. R. Mowbray & Co Ltd,
Saint Thomas House, Becket Street
Oxford, OX1 1SJ

Translated by Emily Chisholm
and the Taizé Community

Originally published in France under the title
Fleurissent les déserts du coeur 1982

All rights reserved. No part of this publication
may be reproduced, stored in a retrieval system,
or transmitted, in any form or by any means,
electronic, mechanical, photocopying, recording,
or otherwise, without the prior permission in writing
from the publisher, A. R. Mowbray & Co. Ltd.

Phototypeset by Wyvern Typesetting Ltd, Bristol

Printed in Great Britain

DEDICATED TO

**Gerhard and Ursula Lange
and their mother
Charlotte Philip**

Contents

Eight pages of black and white photographs
appear between pages 88 and 89.

AND YOUR DESERTS SHALL FLOWER

When desertions, doubts, discouragements and the silences of God seem to cover everything, will you discern the desert flower?

In the desert of your heart, you are sent back to the one thing that matters: giving your life. No one can discover a greater love. And then your whole existence makes sense again.

Didn't you know? In the desert of the heart there were unfailing resources welling up, a life within, an inner light.

To make up this book, a few of my brothers selected from among my notes the texts and prayers for publication. They too were the ones who had the idea of including photographs, and they made the choice.

2

JOURNAL: 1 JANUARY–12 JANUARY 1977

1 January 1977
Since our return from Calcutta, my heart has been full of images: the eyes of the tiny infants, children living in the streets, the look of young women lepers, ravaged by inner loneliness.

After spending time sharing the life of an Asian slum, how can we possibly find some of the conflicts in Europe other than ludicrous? The divisions between Christians, ancient or recent, the misunderstandings between generations, aren't they much ado about nothing? Do the challenges of the Gospel not ring out more directly in surroundings of great poverty, such as the district in Calcutta where we were living?

3 January
On returning to live among my brothers on the hill of Taizé after being away for so long, what strikes one is the intensity of the common prayer. It causes an uprooting of the soul; it unlocks the realities of the Kingdom of God. A period of absence makes the impact of this prayer more evident on return. A breath of life fills it. Why? A detailed analysis

would not give us the answer. Its fullness has grown out of its rhythm and continuity over the years.

At a time when, everywhere in the world, faith and theologies are breaking up into pluralistic currents, the Spirit of the living God is transmitted chiefly through common prayer.

6 January

Every day, several hours go by looking after Marie-Sonaly. She has been sleeping in my room ever since we returned from Calcutta a month ago. A baby of six months old, and so delicate, she would never have survived the winter viruses in Asia. Here, although she is still vomiting too often and is not putting on any weight, she is alive. Sleeping is still a problem. She only falls asleep in my arms. I have learned to write holding her.

10 January

Letter from one of my brothers in Bangladesh. A fire broke out in the shanty town where we stayed with them a short while ago. It was close to their shack. For them it will not be easy to keep from organizing efficacious solutions brought from the West. Their aim is rather to support enterprises launched by local young people and to help them weather discouragements. The people of the neighbourhood have already begun to rebuild what was burned down.

12 January

Could the Gospel be lived out more spontaneously in conditions of extreme poverty? And yet in the northern hemisphere there is a thirst for God, and it is even becoming more intense.

No, our life in Europe has nothing derisory about it. But, seen from Asia, it seemed clearer than ever that the northern hemisphere has vast tracts of spiritual deserts stretching across it. These wastes are the haunts of boredom, disenchantment and a diffuse doubt that leads to scepticism.

FROM DOUBT TO A FINE HUMAN HOPE

From doubt to a fine
human hope

In the northern continents, under the surface there is sometimes a fundamental loneliness, people in the most dire dereliction. Europe and North America have their 'homes for the dying' just as much as Asia, only they are invisible. There are young people, faced with an uncertain future, who even wonder why they were born. When they no longer see the meaning of life, they let themselves drift downhill until mere survival is the only goal they have left.

How can we come to self-fulfilment in God, surrounded as we are by an all-pervasive doubt? How can we move from doubt to hope in God, or at least, for non-believers, from doubt to a fine human hope?

In my journeys to Eastern Europe in recent years I have had the chance to discover that, though the deserts of doubt stretch over the whole northern hemisphere, young Christians in the East perceive them differently from those in the West.

In the East, circumstances lead some of the young Christians – not all of them, of course – to pay more attention than ever to the essential elements of the faith.

9

They find no answer to the doubt around them except in a far-reaching commitment of their lives.

In the West, as far as the quest for God goes, some young people – not all – seem to be driven to prove that they are emancipated. They have so many possibilities as consumers at their disposal, not only of material goods but also of leisure and of culture itself, that they find self-fulfilment only in what captivates them. Dialogue with a view to understanding God sometimes becomes mere chatter about everything under the sun. The most powerful realities of the Gospel are eroded by empty talk. Some of these young people give up the faith in order to be in a solidarity of doubt with non-believers. Taking the easy way out like this is not without effect on the growth of an inner life. Such facile procedures dig a ditch where God disappears.

For anyone seeking fulfilment in Christ, the present situation arouses uneasiness. In both East and West, doubt can attack believers like a kind of subtle, invisible persecution, until they may even begin to think that they have been abandoned by God and his Christ.

In a civilization where doubt is all-pervasive, Christians are deeply affected when they hear it said, among other things, that their faith is only a projection of themselves. The world of doubt becomes corrosive through exclusively cerebral analyses which mean death for the heart.

The temptation of doubt puts our trust in God to the test. It can purify as gold is purified by fire. It can also cast a human being down into the bottom of a well. But there is still always a light shining from above. The darkness is never total. It never invades the whole person completely. God is present even in that darkness.

Harrowed by the trial of doubt, anyone who wants to live the Gospel allows himself to be reborn day after day by the confidence of God. And life finds meaning again.

The meaning of life cannot be drawn from the clouds or from opinions; it is nourished by a confidence. God sends his confidence like a breath of the Spirit falling upon every human being.

One of the irreplaceable marks of the Gospel is that God invites a human being to place his confidence in return in a Man who has come out of the grave and is alive. Faith is not an opinion, it is an attitude: the believer welcomes the Risen Lord and he too becomes alive, not half-dead. Already in the early days of the Church, Irenaeus of Lyons, a Christian of the third generation after Christ – he had known Polycarp who had himself been a disciple of John the Evangelist – wrote: *'The glory of God is a human being fully alive. The life of a human being is the vision of God.'*

Everywhere in the world, large numbers of young people, intent upon prayer, would like to devote their abilities to some generous undertaking. In the depths of their hearts there is a sense of the universal, an aspiration for solidarity with the whole human family, often with its most deprived members. When opportunities are offered, they come running from everywhere. But when such occasions do not arise, some of them slip into excruciating discouragement, the supreme temptation of our day.

For these young people, the future seems a dead end. They feel that the older generation is ready to give them material goods, pocket money, salaries and unemployment benefits, but not to offer them a share in building up society. Since they take so little part in decision-making for the ongoing life of societies and for peace, as well as for the building up of the Church, they withdraw into themselves. Their abilities waste away in obsessive boredom.

Young people of all the nations of the earth are aspiring to build peace. They are ready to stand together and be a ferment of peace, even in places where the human family is being torn apart, whether in the East, the West, the North or the South.

Are they really aware of it? These young people have all they need to overturn determinisms of hatred, war and violence, to restore courage to those who were at the mercy of a diffuse, subtle doubt, and to replace disenchantment with a fine human hope.

PRAYER

Lord Christ, the meaning of our lives lies in your confidence in us. We tell you: 'Lord, I believe, come and help my lack of trust'. And you open for us a way of creation. Along this way, you show us how to create even with our own weaknesses.

Praise to the Risen Christ who, knowing how poor and vulnerable we are, comes and prays in us the hymn of his unchanging confidence.

JOURNAL: 1 FEBRUARY–17 MARCH 1977

1 February
Zurich. Prayer with young people. Although a second church, on the other side of the Limmat, had been linked by telephone wires to the ancient cathedral, young people saw themselves kept out. They were ready to pack in more tightly. Concerned for safety, the police intervened and closed the doors. For a while we heard banging on the doors by those who had been refused entry. Every resounding bang went right to the heart. What's going on? Are the young to be driven away even from a church?

17 February
Spent a long time singing in front of the icon of the Nativity with Marie-Sonaly. At eight months, she is beginning to hold her own. The young woman-doctor who cared for her now admits: 'For more than a month, I thought she would not live.'

18 February

How many women and men think they never do enough for those they love? Their heart condemns them, obstinately.

20 February

'What is forgiveness?' a young Irishman asked me this morning. The most unheard of, the most incredible, the most generous of the realities of the Kingdom of God.

In the crisis of civilization the northern hemisphere is going through, present-day societies are drunk with guilt.

How is it that even Christians make use of the weapons of guilt and suspicion, so contrary to the Gospel? They find it difficult to believe that God has forgiven them. They say to themselves: God forgives others, but not me. Caught up in the vertigo of some indefinable guilt, they would like to begin by forgiving themselves. Unable to do so, they try to escape from their oppression by accusing others.

If we had to love God through fear, through dread of punishment, that would never be love.

Never, never ever, is God a tormentor of a human conscience. The absolute mark of God, writes Saint John, the mystic, is that he is love. And his love, like all love, is first and foremost confident trust and forgiveness.

Christ does not want us drunk with guiltiness, but only filled to overflowing with forgiveness and confidence.

21 February

Continued yesterday's reflections. Too often the Western mind needs an antagonist, to know who was wrong and who was right. Recognizing one's own wrongdoing is considered to be humiliating or an attack on one's dignity.

Forgiveness is so foreign to the human condition; it is a reality of the Kingdom of God where the lukewarm and the cold are excluded.

For anyone who wants to forgive, there is a before and an

after. A before when we say: I was hurt too much as a child, I've been rejected and humiliated all my life, my inner resentment and protest is such that I cannot forgive. And there is an after when, having forgiven, we discover the beginnings of a resurrection on this earth.

Forgiveness: an unequivocal miracle, the extremity of loving. Each time we receive it, we are visited by the living God.

17 March

Leave for Madrid tomorrow. God has entrusted to Spaniards the gift of fire, for them to live the absolute of the Gospel. It is not for nothing that so many mystics and saints have come from Spanish lands. The Spaniards plunge the roots of their faith into deep soil which has been ploughed by trials. They have acquired maturity the hard way. They have the means to light the fire of communion among human beings.

In the course of the Spanish War, I had already made a note in my journal: 'Weep, O my heart, over this people torn apart. Why this calamity, this fratricidal war? Why them?'

With the meeting at Madrid in mind, I prepared a 'letter to a young Spaniard' at Calcutta. Will there be, among the young of this country, witnesses to another future?

LETTER TO A YOUNG SPANIARD

Letter to a young Spaniard

You live in Spanish lands, lands that have always been burning with the passion of a Love, thirsting for the tenderness of God, ravaged by the violence of men, and refreshed at the living waters of the Risen Christ;
you were able to cross the deserts, you knew the silences of God, you went right to the tomb, and that empty tomb did not frighten you;
you knew that he was alive, Christ, the obscure, the poor man, and that at the last day he would stand beside you.
To take the risk of the Gospel today, will you stand beside the Risen Christ, who is in agony for every human being?
You sustain the hope of those who are thirsting for justice: will you radiate the bright light of his communion?

Breath of Christ's loving, fire of his Spirit, kindle the deserts of the heart.
Sweep across them, through every part. Melt all that rebels at the mystery of communion.

Sometimes you ask me where is the source, where is the joy of hoping.

I will answer you.

All your past, even the moment that has just gone by, is already swallowed up, drowned with Christ in the water of your baptism.

Don't look back: that is part of a Christian's freedom. His only interest is running to meet what is to come.

Give up looking back. Not in order to be irresponsible. If you have wounded your neighbour, would you leave him lying on the roadside? Would you refuse reconciliation, refuse to pour oil on his wound?

Give up looking back. Not in order to forget the best of your past. It is up to you to celebrate the times when God passed through your life, to remember your inner liberations.

You will say that to forget the devastations of sin is impossible, no one can do that . . . tenacious, stabbing regrets remain.

If your imagination brings back destructive memories of the past, at least be aware that God, for his part, takes no account of them.

Have you understood? One of the greatest risks in living Christ for others is forgiveness. To forgive and forgive again, that is what wipes out the past and plunges you into the present moment.

Christian, you bear the name of Christ: for you every moment can become fullness of life.

The word love is so often abused. Living out a love that forgives is another matter.

You can never forgive out of self-interest, to change the other person. That would be a miserable calculation which has nothing to do with the free gift of love. You can only forgive because of Christ.

You will dare to pray with Jesus his last prayer:

'Father, forgive them: they do not know what they are doing.' And spontaneously this second prayer will arise: 'Father, forgive me: so often I don't know what I am doing either.'

Forgiving means even refusing to take into account what the other will do with your forgiveness.

Forgiving: there lies the secret stimulus that will make you too a witness to a different future.

PRAYER

O living God, show us how to turn to you at every moment.
So often we forget that your Holy Spirit lives in us, prays in us, loves in us.
Your miracle in us is your continual forgiveness, and our confidence in you.
O living God, here and now, in the present moment, 'you disperse our faults like morning mist,' and slip on our finger the ring of the prodigal son.

JOURNAL: 20 MARCH–27 MAY 1977

20 March

At Madrid, with young people from all over the country. We searched for ways of making forgiveness concrete. I remembered that, when I was very young, it seemed to me necessary not to keep letters and papers through which bitterness could be cultivated. Since then, I burn almost everything as we go along; we keep no archives. Nations have mountains of archives. To burn all the papers where hatred and the memory of an offence are preserved is an action which prepares for forgiveness.

21 March

A youth from Madrid asks: how can a reconciliation come about when the other refuses?

That refusal is like a little death which makes us lose our footing. It is not easy for anybody to pick themselves up again. Nothing hurts so deeply as to find someone with whom we are seeking reconciliation cold and distant. Our heart is wounded to the very depths.

It can even happen that forgiveness leads the other to this

cynical calculation: why not go on further with my plan, even to the point of trampling the other person underfoot, because in any case he will pardon me for Christ's sake?

If the other persists in his refusal, does that mean that God does not answer prayer? Actually God has already answered 'in ourselves'. His answer was given 'within us'; he has already reconciled us within.

30 March

Phone call from Rumania. Two young people had set out from here to take help to the earthquake victims; they announce the death of Justinian, the much-loved patriarch. Against wind and tide, that man did everything in his power to allow the Orthodox Church of Rumania to come through her trials.

31 March

For the last three years, an old established publishing house has been asking to compile a book consisting of conversations in the course of which I would have to answer many questions. We chose the journalist. He came twice to interview me. Gradually I realized that we were preparing a book where I would constantly have to express myself in the first person. My blood froze at the prospect. Everything within me urged me to give up the project, to return to it later perhaps, at a more advanced age.

2 May

If the springtime of the Church cannot come about here and now, God at least gives it to us within ourselves. He does not refuse us a springtime of the heart.

14 May

Meeting with Paul VI. He listened with close attention and was interested in our experiences with the young people in Calcutta. At one point, he said: 'I would not like to fail these young people who take commitment so far.' Later: 'I would like to be worthy of them.' Then he asked: 'What can I do for them?' His candour goes to one's heart. Looking at this man who has been devastated by trials, a word sprung spontaneously to my lips: 'Most Holy Father, I see in you marks of the holiness of Christ.'

22 May

Although the little wood, tamed by the paths Eric has cleared, tumbles down almost perpendicularly into the valley of the Grosne, its solitude is inviting. Against the wall, at midday, in the shade of slender sycamore trees, white carpets under the leaves: here the wild garlic is coming up after the violets. And already the grasses are getting ready to rise. A wave of heat has fallen over the countryside. It would be wonderful to follow the quickening rhythm of the vegetation every day. The sheer bounty of the so-called wild flowers, those that grow up walls, between two stones, is so appealing.

24 May

Some of my young brothers are passionately interested in the Scriptures. This afternoon, a few of us were talking about some almost incomprehensible Gospel sayings. How to make them understandable to young people?

Those words cannot be taken in isolation. The Gospel can only be considered as a whole. Just as each of us wishes to be appreciated in the context of his whole life, and not in one isolated situation, in the same way it is important to see the words of the Bible in the context of Scripture as a whole.

Very often, we approach Scripture as if we were reading a letter from someone we love above all else, but who is writing

25

to us in an unknown tongue. We try to translate at least a few words, the simplest ones if possible. What remains inaccessible in the Gospel, we can just leave alone. Later on, others will help us to understand.

26 May
Each one of us carries within himself a great inner theme. Let it sing and go on singing. It is useless to look elsewhere. A continuous creation is born of that.

27 May
Under the trees, in the dusk, intense happiness came and went. The house, with its four lighted windows, seemed to me the most welcoming place on earth. This morning, leaning against the garden wall reading, the very same happiness. Does it come from man? I have no idea. But it goes straight to God.

THE SECRET OF A HAPPINESS

The secret of a happiness

How can we face up to the difficulties of life? By constantly turning our steps back towards the essential. And we can discover the essential only through the heart, or what comes to the same thing, through the depths.

How can we keep going? By daring to move forward after every discouragement, after every failure. Not with an ideal heart, but with the one we have. Not with the heart we don't have: God will change it.

God's radiance shines through human vulnerability. When a human being can see no solutions, all he can do is to abandon himself to God, in body and spirit. If he were not so destitute, he would perhaps not be searching so passionately for creative strength in God.

Our weaknesses make us more sensitive to our neighbour, more inclined to create together with others. So-called strong persons imprison themselves in authoritarianism and paralyse everybody around them.

The day comes when we glimpse the secret of a happiness. It is not outside of ourselves; the Kingdom is within.

In every human being areas almost impossible to reach

lie dormant. Sometimes they hurt us. They are like a vast universe inhabited by a host of contradictory forces, originating perhaps in ancestral memories, whether explicit or not, as well as from childhood memories.

These cross-currents can shut us up in inner prisons. If we visit these prisons in the company of Christ, in the course of a life-long inner pilgrimage, suddenly the walls come tumbling down. In their place unfold vistas of freedom. To our surprise, a whole universe of torments has evaporated.

Why worry about a flood of inner tears? There will always be a Noah's ark on the waters, to praise the living God.

Human beings stop short at outward appearances. God sees not the surface, but the heart. He gives us the gift of discerning, beyond the contradictions, the secret of a happiness.

Waiting for you, O Christ, in the company of the Virgin Mary and the apostles, waiting for you, when all is immersed in the silence of God, waiting for you and discovering at any age, in the hollow of the heart, a source of freshness: your confidence, and the spirit of simplicity.

To each one of us, you speak the same language: 'Look, I am here, at the heart of your solitude as well as in your times of joy and serenity. You are waiting for me and searching for me, so look: here I am. Why do you doubt? I have already met you.'

JOURNAL: 31 MAY–16 SEPTEMBER 1977

31 May
A 'parable of community' can be recognized when it speaks for itself and can be understood without any explanations. When I was very young, I was deeply aware of this at a time when I was confronted with this alternative: either to be a writer (while living in the country), expressing myself primarily with my pen; or else foster the creation of a 'parable of community'. In the end, the decision came of its own accord. May this parable be able to speak for itself!

2 June
Letter from Finland. It mentions the arrival of young people who set out from here: 'It would be good if they could go on as far as Lapland. As for ourselves, we have just spent a few days in Lithuania. Christians there send you their greetings.'

Do they realize all they are bringing with them, these young people who, after a time of preparation, come and go from one country to another, in the East as in the West?

6 June
In the village where I lived as a child, the Christians went on

Sundays to pray in two different places. Some went to a church, the others to a hall. They even passed each other in the street. Our family admired as saintly women some of those who went to pray in the other place. It was impossible to be together, and yet we loved one another so much! Could the misfortune of the Christians of that village be one of the motives that led me later on to want to live with others a parable of community? Happy experiences are not the only ones that stimulate creation . . .

4 July
Saw once again tonight a boy who talked to me last year about an inner drama. Fortunately, if I forget the names, I do remember faces and words well enough.

His suffering goes on and on. There is nothing more cruel than a love rejected or broken off. The heart does not know how to react and, sometimes, as a way of defending itself against too much suffering, it grows hard. And then an antidote arises: self-love. From humiliation that is not accepted, the pride of life and human ambition are born.

When Christ is rejected, he does not rebel. He suffers and he loves.

5 July
Moving letter in the mail from Amédée, one of the twenty boys who found a home here in the village when they were very young. My sister Genevieve became their mother. He writes:

> 'I have so many worries and so much work. I get up at five o'clock to look after my animals and to do my work properly. The doctor says I'm straining at the leash too much. But tomorrow is in God's hands; all I can do is live one day at a time. I often repeat: my real family is at Taizé, that's where my heart is. That's what I tell my children.'

6 August

Fifteen years ago today, our 'Church of Reconciliation' was inaugurated. In this connection there is a story that should really be written down for once.

About 1947, the mother of a family told me that as she was walking along, praying, she came to the end of the village and had a vision of a high cross that had been set up. She insisted on pointing out the exact spot. Her tale embarrassed me and I never spoke of it. In 1960, the time came to build a church. I wanted it to be close to our house. Several of my brothers preferred it to be at a distance and that is what was done. A long time afterwards I realized that it had been built on the spot where that woman had seen a cross standing.

What can one make of these coincidences?

15 August

Bishop Romero, of San Salvador, wrote to me recently to ask me to intervene with the President of his country on the basis of a dossier that came with his letter.

Addressed today a message to the President of El Salvador, including these lines:

> 'Many young people are deeply concerned about what has been happening in El Salvador. Father Rutilio Grande and two peasant catechists have been assassinated in their church by the army. Father Alfonso Navarro was killed in his house along with a young layman. Other priests have been imprisoned and tortured, and a campaign of slander has been maintained against the Catholic Church.
>
> Young Christians are conscience-stricken by these facts. In the name of human dignity, I appeal to the Christianity you profess, in order that you will take measures for such events to cease on Salvadorian soil. I am confident in the Risen Christ, who is knocking at the door of your human heart.'

17 August

All through the summer months, together with some of the young people, we have been asking ourselves what it means to live dangerously for the sake of Christ.

To travel far and join the poorest, is that living dangerously? Yes, but that's not all there is to it. Giving one's body to be burned, sharing one's goods, committing one's energies in the struggle for justice, is that living dangerously? Expending all one's strength to take part in the birth of a new humanity, could that be it, living dangerously? Yes, but that's not all there is to it. These commitments may be undertaken without a burning love.

Who, then, lives dangerously? The one who goes with Jesus through death to resurrection and is willing, with him, to give up even life for love.

30 August

At fifteen months, Marie-Sonaly already loves to have her meals in company. This evening she was present at the meal alone with me and an African bishop who was passing through. She sat on my knees for a while then slid to the ground, under the table, to go to the bishop. It didn't take me long to understand what attracted her. The bishop wore a cassock with a long row of buttons and, as the little girl was teething, she was chewing on the buttons!

31 August

Repeated to a girl from Belgium who spoke of her deep unhappiness: anyone who looks only at himself will inevitably sink into melancholy. Open your eyes to creation all around you, and the shadows already begin to disperse.

12 September

Invited to speak at the eucharistic congress in Pescara. To the

Italians I love so much, I want to say that God has placed in the Catholic Church a vocation to be a ferment of communion for the whole human race. They are so close to Rome, are they aware that their attention to the Bishop of Rome's ministry of universality has far-reaching consequences?

For four and a half centuries now, one part of Christendom has been fleeing the Bishop of Rome.

Christ entrusted the Church to Peter. Does the universal pastor have any choice? Is he not the pastor of all the baptized, even of those, Catholics or not, who do not understand his ministry? Is it not his vocation to be an ecumenical pastor, not only for part of the baptized, but for all of them?

As for those around him, his co-workers, we can see that the younger generations have definite expectations regarding them. They wish this little land of liberty, the Vatican, would offer a welcome that is simple but warm, a welcome as wide as the world.

15 September
At Pescara we stayed in a working-class neighbourhood, in the home of simple people, Marcello's parents. His mother was the epitome of the joy of living. In the midst of the hullabaloo of the family, she said: 'Nothing is more beautiful than the day of my death; I will rest in God for all eternity.'

16 September
One of the questions we are asked most often: why do so many young Europeans come to Taizé? My brothers and I sometimes say: we really don't know why; God will tell us on the day we meet him face to face in the life of eternity.

When, every evening, winter and summer, a few of us stay on in the church to listen to young people one at a time, our concern is: what lies underneath their hearts? What is tying them up in knots? What are their inner prisons? And then a

36

still more important necessity appears: what are their particular gifts? How can they discover them?

We know that they have not come here as tourists. If so, they would have come to the wrong address. Most of them have come with one and the same question: how can I understand God? How can I know what God wants for me?

If they have come, those who are thirsting for the living God, it is to take stock of themselves, to question themselves in the silence of their own hearts, in order to try to follow Christ.

THE RADIANCE OF GOD'S OWN FACE

The radiance of God's own face

'You are the God of all human beings, and since the dawn of time, you have inscribed within each person a law of love. But few there are who realize that you have created us in your image, free to love.

God, the living God, in your striving to make yourself understood, you came to earth in Christ Jesus as one of the poor.

And this Jesus, rejected, tortured on a cross, dead and laid in a tomb, you raised to life again.'

No one can understand the death of Jesus without knowing him first as the Risen Lord. Then, in a flash, we glimpse the mystery:

'O Christ, you ask us the very same question you asked your disciples: "Who do you say I am?"

You are the One who is alive. Risen from the dead, you are in agony with all who are afflicted. Your Spirit lives in everyone who undergoes human suffering.

You call upon each of us to follow you. And following you means taking up our own cross every day. But you come down to where we are, down to the very depths, to take upon yourself all that weighs us down. You remain alongside each one of us. You even go and visit those who died before they could possibly know you (1 Peter 3.19–20).

The contemplation of your boundless mercy becomes a radiant goodness in the humble hearts that let themselves be led by your Spirit.'

That God, through Christ, should make himself so universal is far beyond the ability of the human mind to comprehend. Confronted with such a great mystery, a man in the Gospel cried out: 'Lord, I believe; come and help my weak faith.' And this little scrap of faith, the little bit that each one discovers day after day, turns out to be enough to advance in the steps of the Risen Christ.

Anyone who wants to follow Christ places his confidence in him, on days when the heart is full just as at times when it cries out in loneliness.

'If you were not risen, Lord Christ, to whom could we go to find the radiance of God's own face?

If you were not risen, we would not be together seeking your communion. We would not find forgiveness and reconciliation at your side – those wellsprings of a new beginning.

If you were not risen, where could we draw the energy to follow you to the very end of our lives, choosing you again and again, even in old age?'

Choosing Christ! He confronts us with an alternative: 'Whoever would save his life will lose it. Whoever gives his life for love of me will find it.' But he does not impose the choice. He leaves each one free to choose him or to reject him. He never forces us. Simply, gentle and humble of heart, he has been standing for two thousand years at the door of every human heart and knocking: 'Do you love me?'

When it seems that the ability to respond to him has disappeared, we can only call out: 'Give me the gift to give myself, to rest in you, O Christ, in body and in spirit.'

Choosing Christ means walking on one road only, not on two roads at the same time. Anyone who wants both to follow Christ and to follow himself would be setting out to follow his own shadow, in pursuit of reputation or social prestige. In his desire to serve himself, would such a person even unconsciously go so far as to make Christ and that communion which is the Church a tool of his own purposes?

Looking back after having consented to the call does not leave one unscathed. Regrets feed anxiety and rebellion against oneself. Like waves, in the end they flood over the dike of the self and move towards others. And then what devastation!

For anyone who is trying to run away, nothing is more essential than to be listened to. Never keep to yourself what is wounding you deep down. Don't remain half-dead. Dare to tell everything to someone else, someone who has gone through trials, has made use of intuition and has learned to read what lies under the surface, without passing judgement.

The day will come again when you can whisper:

'In my longing to live nothing but the one essential, I remember you, the Risen Christ. My heart, my mind, my body are like dry ground, thirsting for you. I had forgotten you, but all the time I kept on loving you. And you shower on me a love called forgiveness; you bring me to life.'

JOURNAL: 17 SEPTEMBER 1977–1 JANUARY 1978

17 September

Speaking to everybody in the church tonight, an old Orthodox bishop, uncommonly generous of heart, said emphatically: 'Every human being is inhabited by the Holy Spirit.' As he is a bit hard of hearing, he shouted to Jean-François, who was standing by his side: 'Have they really understood what I said? Every human being is inhabited by the Holy Spirit.'

18 September

We had our meal outdoors with the Orthodox bishop. A stiff breeze from the distant ocean was raising waves in the leafy maples. All through the meal I kept looking at my brothers, and I marvelled. So many faces and behind them talents that are unique and lives that have been offered!

25 September

Visit from a young African. He has been living in exile for

six years now and has no news at all of his family. Not knowing how to express adequately all that his presence means, I ventured to say to him: since you are not only the stranger but the exile as well, it is you who will sit at the head of the table. You will welcome us to the meal; our home is yours.

17 October

How often when I was a child did I hear these words: 'Don't stand there doing nothing. Play or work, but do something.' Obediently, I would look for things to do. In the autumn of my life something of that lives on. Just like a little horse pulling on his collar, pulling, pulling and pulling, till he falls to his knees by dint of pulling.

18 October

Asish has just arrived. This young Hindu is an active volcano. A fire burns within him. Last year, when he learned that we were going to stay in a slum in Calcutta, he spent two weeks looking for us. As he is worried about the young people in his city, he wants us to return with him and live in Calcutta. We share the confident belief that God, since the dawn of time, has been trying to respond to the secret thirst in human beings by telling them: 'I love you with an everlasting love.'

3 November

The rain keeps on falling. The lakes it has made turn the flooded valley into a Finnish landscape. But it's a Finland without the disadvantages – no ice on the roads, and carpets of leaves the tender green colour of early spring.

6 November

Vienna Cathedral. Prayer with young Austrians on the eve of the departure for Asia.

Going to the gates of China . . .

For the younger generations, the borders that tear humanity apart are almost intolerable. At a time when suspicion and a crisis of confidence are predominant in the world, we are going to that frontier to pray for confident trust among all peoples. Young people from each continent are already there. We will set out with no plans, to live with the poorest of the poor and to understand what God is trying to say through them.

9 November

Hong Kong. The bus passes through the densely populated old city. Everywhere, high-rise buildings for one family per room under construction. Everything gives the impression of overcrowding, even the street.

We find a place to stay on the sea, next to some 'Little Sisters of Jesus'. Like many of the poor, they live on a junk in a 'floating district'. On the edge of the area, a family is about to move to a better place. This family agrees to leave us their shack, built on tall piles driven into the water. The way in is by a hole a meter high, in the wire fence surrounding the floating district. This hole is the only entrance for the inhabitants of hundreds of boats and shacks.

Here, the 'street' is the water, criss-crossed by little boats continually coming and going. Our shanty is made of flotsam and jetsam, bits of used planks and crates. When the tide rises, it sways gently. No electricity. Drinking water has to be fetched by boat.

10 November

With straw matting, bowls, a stove for the kitchen and two oil lamps the shack, with all its odd bits and pieces, already has an atmosphere of harmony. Sunlight plays on the matting, with lively reflections from the water. Starting today a young Chinese priest is going to share our life. Every evening he will celebrate the Eucharist in his own tongue.

46

11 November

The reserved Sacrament has been placed below the icon of Christ. In the poverty of this place there will now be a corner of rare beauty. Irresistibly we are drawn there to pray. The cramped conditions demand a simple, unified life with no separation between prayer and the various activities.

12 November

Every evening we are together for an hour of sharing in the makeshift dormitory. We spread our blankets and sleep on the floor. Thinking that at my age I would never adjust to a dormitory, I wanted them to find me a little place where I could sleep alone. It was not possible.

Yesterday at mealtime huge rats appeared. When we tried to chase them, one turned round like a cat ready to scratch. In the evening, the din of the rats started up again. People explained to us that it was better to leave an oil-lamp burning all night; that would keep them from biting. As a matter of fact, they sometimes run over our bodies.

13 November

We look down on the first of the junks where three children, Chan, Kun and Meng, smile at us all day long. They are more reserved than the children of Calcutta. Their mother suffers from meningitis; she looks haggard. The smallest is tied to a post to keep him from falling into the water. With his little hand he continually throws us kisses. At this very moment he is washing himself skilfully. When he starts to cry we jump into our little boat to go over and comfort him. One of the little girls has the face of an icon. Black eyes, features barely indicated, hair well cut by the father into a fringe on her brow. Human beauty pure and simple.

This family epitomizes the whole of the Chinese people. Praying for them is a way of praying for all Chinese everywhere. Surrounded by non-believers, everything tells us: wherever there is a human being, God is present. The

47

Church is so much wider than the human mind can imagine. In the heart of God the Church is as vast as humankind.

15 November

The young Asians in our group have expressed the wish that, in the afternoon after our discussion, we could say the rosary. They have been brought up on this prayer. Each says it in his or her mother-tongue – Chinese, Bengali, Marathi, Thai, Indonesian, Filipino and in the European languages. We find that it is possible to insert spontaneous intercessions into this age-old prayer which is the angel's greeting to Mary (after the words '. . . and blessed is the fruit of thy womb, Jesus' we say 'and in him are blessed . . .' adding the names of those we wish to pray for).

16 November

A few young Chinese have come to live with us. Some of them have the opportunity of going to visit their families in mainland China.

Our group is no elite. Clear thinking is not our strong point. But are our hearts not childlike? At any rate, the letter to be written together will be a spontaneous one.

17 November

The side of the shack facing the junks is completely open, with no partition. At night we hang up plastic sacks sewn together. In the daytime, impossible to make a move without being seen by people passing in boats. And we ourselves are continually caught up in the life unfolding before our eyes.

The women dress austerely – trousers, a huge straw hat which partly conceals their faces, often a child clinging to their backs. The cloth-merchant passes by in a little boat, calling at junk after junk. On another boat the fruit-woman shouts her wares. We are awakened at dawn by the baker's voice, selling his bread.

A visitor tells us: living with the boat-people, you are at the very heart of the Chinese.

18 November

Last night the thermometer fell sharply from thirty-two to fifteen degrees Celsius. A typhoon in the Philippines had created a rush of cold air from the continent. A violent wind blew all night long. The hut was creaking all over. It seemed to be disintegrating in the buffeting gusts. But the piles held.

Our living conditions are more rigorous than last year in Calcutta. Human beings' capacity for adaptation is astonishing.

20 November

As the shack gets more and more crowded with visitors coming and going, an old junk, lent by neighbours, was to serve as our place of prayer beginning today. This morning we had just arrived and were already on our knees, when a woman jumped from her boat towards us. She was shouting. We did not understand what she wanted until we noticed that we were sinking. We had to leave as quickly as possible. When they sink, junks are swallowed up instantly by the sea.

21 November

On the junk opposite, a curious ceremonial: the grandmother is offering a sacrifice to their ancestors. The flame of her offering is the only light in the darkness.

22 November

The little daughter of one of our neighbours fell into the water and drowned. She was four. The heart bleeds.

24 November

As we toil away on the letter to be published on our return, the question arises once more: why express anything in writing when the best of a pastoral ministry seems to be lived out in conversations face to face?

25 November

Our text has found its final form. It will be a 'letter to all generations.' We read it tonight with the young Chinese who had come for the prayer. Will this letter show clearly enough that all segregation creates a split in the inner life of the human being?

28 November

The workmen on a neighbouring site shared our meal. They come from mainland China and return there regularly. They have never had an invitation like this, they said. They see us at prayer every day: one of them pointed a finger to the sky to say he understood what that meant.

29 November

Why come out here on the China Sea to share the life of the most neglected? It is not a question of personal taste, or of a natural inclination; it is to allow the most trying human conditions to enter into our own lives. It is dangerous to appeal for solidarity with the poor while staying at home and doing nothing.

30 November

Last night fire broke out among the junks. We were still up, and we wakened those who had already gone to sleep. Anguished cries from those whose junks were on fire. Some threw themselves into the sea. Nobody died, but some were injured, and about fifty boats destroyed.

This morning, a few of us went in a little boat from one junk to the next, the ones spared by the fire where the shipwrecked families had been taken in. We all love one another. An ocean of goodness shines on their faces.

These non-believers have a Presence dwelling within them. Surrounded by these Chinese people, we are convinced of one thing: wherever they may be, every human being is visited by the Spirit of God.

In the western world, too, so many men and women experience the silence of God. The night seems dark and they wonder: 'Where can God be?' To us, living on the China Sea, it is becoming evident that God's silence is only apparent. Christ stands at the door, knocking. He is close beside each one of us, including those who do not even know his name.

4 December

On our way home, visit to a camp of Vietnamese refugees in Thailand. Welcomed at a country hospital by an old French nun, we discover she was born not far from Taizé. She is so human that we say: we have found a true sister of Pope John XXIII!

Then, although we had no inkling of it when we entered the camp, the necessity was borne upon us to prepare to receive Indochinese widows and their children. I remember that everything began in Taizé with the welcome of political refugees. From the very start I was convinced: the more exacting our prayer becomes, the more it leads us to enter into the critical situations of humankind.

24 December

Along with a Christmas card, the Pope sent an Italian cake, a *panettone*, to us at Taizé.

At the beginning of this month, on our return from the China Sea, Max was waiting for me in Rome. He had prepared everything so well, we were able to go together right away to put the 'letter to all generations' into the Pope's own hands. Paul VI said at that time: 'During the weeks you spent in Asia, I was praying for you.'

1 January 1978

In this year just beginning, what gestures can we find to make it clear how necessary it is for Christians to be reconciled without delay?

In this connection I thought again about a recent conversation with a leading Protestant on his way through Taizé. We only had a few moments together. To help him understand the meaning of our vocation as quickly as possible, I told him the story of my grandmother. His reaction was immediate; for him that story shed light on our whole quest. Why didn't I dare speak of it sooner?

My mother's mother was a woman of courage. During the First World War her three sons were fighting at the front. She was a widow and she lived in the North of France, where they were under shell-fire. But she insisted on staying, so that she could open her home to refugees – old people, children, pregnant women. She did not leave till the last minute when everyone had to flee. Then she went to the Dordogne.

She was penetrated by the deep desire that never again would anyone have to go through what she had experienced. In Europe, divided Christians were killing one another; let them at least be reconciled, to prevent another war.

She came from old Protestant stock: in the house where my mother was born, guests were still shown the secret chamber where in times past the pastor was hidden during periods of persecution. To bring about an immediate reconciliation within herself, she used to go to a Catholic Church. It was as if she had known intuitively that, in the Catholic Church, the Eucharist was a source of unanimity of the faith.

The miracle of her life was that in reconciling within herself the stream of her original faith with the Catholic faith, she did not become a symbol of repudiation for her family.

She arrived at my parents' a year or so later. Worn out with fatigue, she fainted as she entered our house. They carried her away in a red blanket. I can see the scene as if it had just taken place.

This made a great impact on me and something irreversible took place. Those two gestures of hers – taking in the most distressed and achieving a reconciliation within oneself – had a life-long effect upon me.

My grandmother's intuition must have given me a Catholic soul from childhood. I have the impression that, at Taizé, I have continued along the road opened up by that elderly lady. In her footsteps, I found my own identity by reconciling in my depths the stream of faith of my origins with the faith of the Catholic Church, without however being a symbol of repudiation for anyone in the process.

Mothers or grandmothers can rejoice. Their acts of faithfulness sometimes leave traces whose total results will never be seen in their lifetimes.

RECONCILIATION, WITHOUT DELAY

Reconciliation, without delay

Reconciliation: not to be stronger against anyone, never in a crusading spirit, but in order to be a ferment of confidence for both believers and non-believers.

Why this inconsistency among Christians, separated not only by ancient divisions but by quite recent ones too? Could they dare waste a single minute arguing with one another, when violence and rumours of war are spreading over the world?

Christ is torn apart in the Christian family.

The Gospel is disinterestedness at its purest. It does not call Christians to win a following, but to be members of the Body of Christ. Denominational separations tend to make Christians into partisans, or even 'patriots', of their confession.

Only a reconciliation can resolve a latent crisis and permit an awakening and a springtime of the Church.

In other dark periods of history, Christians were able to visit one another in order to bridge the gaps. Mural paintings attest that at difficult times in the thirteenth century, Christians in Southern Europe would travel as far as Finland. They would undertake this kind of little pilgrimage in small groups, from one individual to another, from group to group.

At the beginning of the Second Vatican Council, it

seemed that unity between separated churches was about to come to pass. This did not happen. Today, leaders of Christian confessions do not hide the fact that it will take several decades to resolve the structural questions raised by ecumenism.

The ecumenical process has widened theological research through meetings and commissions. It has not been without importance that Christians are recognizing one another in their differences and then letting the convergences appear. But that is not yet reconciliation.

An ecumenical dialogue will be essential until the end of time. Even if Christians were reunited in one Church, opposite tendencies would always appear, needing time in which to search for the spirit of unity.

For all that, it is impossible to forget that in the Gospel reconciliation is a dynamic of the here-and-now, of the immediate present, of every moment: 'If you are on your way to the altar, unreconciled, first of all run and be reconciled with your brother.'

Whereas ecclesial institutions may need a great deal of time to enter into visible communion, following the Gospel's road of immediacy, each person can anticipate reconciliation within themselves, and do so without delay.

Anticipating is an expression of hope. It means living out already what one is hoping for. Nothing is better for keeping the heart young and alert, until the very evening of life.

When, after a separation, the one who has swallowed his pride and gone to the other hears in reply: 'I wish you well, but I have everything I need; what can you give me?' it is humiliating. On the one hand forgiveness, on the other self-sufficiency.

To anticipate a reconciliation, will you begin,

without delay, to make your own the best of the gifts Christ Jesus has placed in his people during their two thousand years of pilgrimage? Following this way no one will ever tear the fibres of the soul of their own family nor become a symbol of repudiation.

Making our very own the best of the gifts of the Orthodox Churches means entrusting oneself to the Spirit of the Risen Lord. He shines through in the liturgy to such an extent that non-believers can sense his presence. It is there that Orthodox Christians have drawn courage faithfully to go to the very extreme of loving.

Making one's own the best of the Reformation Churches means trusting in the Word of God, in order to put it into practice in one's personal life. Love of the Scriptures has forged the very soul of Reformation Christians. Out of meditation on Scripture they have developed spontaneous prayer, that treasure of the Gospel, expressing intercession for others or thankfulness to God.

Making one's own the best of the gifts of the Catholic Church means opening oneself to the irreplaceable presence of the Risen Christ in the Eucharist, and receiving as well the forgiveness given at the source of reconciliation. Drawing from the Word of God a certainty confirmed by the centuries, the Catholic Church is above all the Church of the Eucharist. In the Eucharist, source of unanimity of one and the same faith, a breath of continuity makes it possible to pass through even the most difficult trials in the course of history. And the Eucharist opens us to a mystical vision of the Church; it can even provide a mystical vision of the human being.

PRAYER

You are the God of all the peoples of the earth,
and in your Christ you reconcile all things to
yourself, so that nothing is disastrous except the
loss of love.
Lord Christ, in your presence we are sometimes
at a loss: you dwell in us, and we dwell in you.
Come, Spirit of the Risen Christ, on those days
when reconciliation involves an inner combat.
Come and sing within us, and lift us up by your
confidence in us.

JOURNAL: 6 JANUARY–13 MAY 1978

6 January
The simplicity of life in Asia is leading us to look for ways of simplifying our own life here. There, we discovered that sleeping in a dormitory could be a night spent with Christ. Why not try it here? Our brothers from the southern hemisphere have never known anything else than a single room for the whole family. Pierino, our youngest brother, with his typically Italian generosity, spreads infectious joy in the dormitory. The icon stays lit all night long. It is like a vigil with Christ . . .

7 January
This year the annual council-meeting of the community is a common celebration of our vocation and a meditation on the world today. Within the community, our gifts express themselves in such different ways. The silent or the shy are by no means absent members; sometimes it is they who inspire us most.

9 January

At the council-meeting, we say once again that our fraternities, in the southern and northern continents, are not 'foundations'. That idea is foreign to us. In order to live a parable of reconciliation we are a single family, made up of brothers of different confessions, races and cultures.

In the human community, exacerbated by new forms of segregation, antagonisms can only be resolved in a mixing of races and cultures. Certainly mixing only leads to communion if it draws its life from the same sources: the same faith, the same vocation.

The little book which expresses the essential elements we hold in common is improperly called our 'rule'. It is neither a constitution nor a legal document. Would it not be better to speak of the 'sources of Taizé'?

2 February

After the 25th of December and Epiphany, today we are celebrating a third Christmas, that of the offering. Following an ancient tradition, a little donkey was brought into the church. A symbol of the poverty of Jesus, an image of Christ who takes everything upon his shoulders. In these long winters a series of festivals, one after another, is so welcome.

6 February

On the eve of Frank's departure for Asia, we share our thoughts around the fire. 'We would not be able to keep coming and going from one continent to another,' he says, 'if we did not all have common roots here, in one place. In order to keep going when we are far away, we have to constantly deepen our love for this place, given to us by God.'

18 February

For the season of Lent dried leaves have been strewn in the

church near the icon of the Virgin. From time to time I give out a few of them to people to signify that, when he forgives us again and again, God is inviting us to blow away remorse itself like a child blowing an autumn leaf. We can be sure of one thing: where there is forgiveness, God is there, always.

23 February

In New York, Leonard, with his rare intuition, found on the fifth floor of a building just what we were looking for: a ruin of an apartment, with a broken roof, in a violent neighbourhood with a Hispanic majority. Brothers will go to live there. Before they left, we were asking ourselves: what will their life be? A simple life, imbued with the Gospel. But how is it possible to mix with the dough of humanity without becoming so secular that we cease to be bearers of signs of Christ? In recent years Christians have believed that they had to abandon the visible signs of the Gospel in order to become part of a human community. Very often they gradually stopped praying.

25 February

Is it the sheer 'folly of the Gospel' which brings us to envisage the possibility of several of our brothers leaving for distant lands? And yet here there has to be a certain number of us present to take care of growing needs.

1 March

Wrote to someone close to me, on the eve of an important day:

> 'When the humiliated man in you would like to shake off everything he considers a dead weight, don't forget that this weight may be the easy yoke of Christ, his arm around your shoulders. When the stranglehold of rebellion makes you despair to the

point of forsaking the Christ who called you once and for all, return to the inner oasis, the place of solitude within yourself; there, he repeats over and over again the same call. Of you he asks much – he has richly blessed you with gifts. Do not cast away these precious pearls by wasting your energies in finding out who was right and who was wrong. Let your life be a response of wonder at all he has placed within you.'

2 March

The first crocuses are sparkling, little splashes of bright gold set in the hollow of a shrub. In the wood, primroses have been in flower since January. Caught unawares by the north wind of these last two days, their corollas crumple up, stifled.

10 March

Letter from a youth of seventeen:

'My parents are atheists, so I never had occasion to ask myself questions about faith till I was thirteen or fourteen. Today I am asking myself questions. I read the Bible but it did not convince me at all. I went to Mass and there I was moved more than I have ever been before. I felt as if I had been touched by the grace of God. From then on I began to believe and, one day, I felt the need to meet someone who could help me understand the faith.'

A significant letter. The way young people today approach faith has changed profoundly. In former days one began with the catechism and then moved towards Eucharistic communion. Today many young people have had little or no religious instruction. But some sense something of the mystery of Christ's presence when, on going into a Catholic Church, they hear a celebration of the Eucharist and, one day, take part in it.

For these young people, then, the Eucharist is not the end of their road to faith, but the beginning. The Eucharist was the first thing that touched them, and they receive it in all seriousness.

12 March

Letter from Eric, one of our brothers living in New York, a few weeks after their arrival in the Hispanic neighbourhood:

'It's not simple living in a dirty, gloomy house, with so little room. But we are overwhelmed by the friendship of our neighbours. In the heart of fragmented New York, we measure to what extent no half-measures are possible: our vocation can only be radical.'

This brother does not add what I learned from another source: in this time of extreme cold in New York, their apartment is not heated.

16 March

Marie-Sonaly brings me her first bunch of flowers, daisies; she lays them in my hands. Her big black eyes shine with happiness.

30 March

The young people stay in the church longer and longer. Before the common prayer they are there ahead of time. Afterwards they stay on as if the prayer had no end to it. A few of us brothers have begun to stay on with them, singing hymns repeated over and over as if to infinity.

In our beginnings, we worked out a prayer that was mainly monastic. Then, in order to come closer to the People of God, we endeavoured to make it meditative and accessible at the same time, congenial to all generations and as universal as possible.

May it help people to discover the universal heart of

the Church and an intense longing for the Kingdom of God . . .

18 April
On rising, a light haze blurred the landscape, making the trees mere silhouettes. The mist, warmed by the barely concealed sun, caressed the earth with soft gauze.

22 April
Very often a man or a woman who dared to pray alone in a church has been, by their perseverance, a living appeal to others. It only takes one, for many to be drawn along in the end.

24 April
My sister Renée's birthday. Since my tender infancy, a red-letter day. Renée, she was the laughing one, the daring one. Now, over seventy, she is just the same. When a generous project is afoot, nothing can stop her.

28 April
In the train to Bari with fifteen young brothers, going to spend some time in a working-class parish. In Italy, the situation has worsened. For us, it is as if members of our own family were having a hard time. It is good to join them.

The train has stopped in the middle of the countryside. Landscape filled with the freshness of spring. Down the slope from the track, cherry trees laden with small green fruits, fig trees with lavish foliage. On the other side, arid mountains. Where do the sheep find a few tufts of grass?

The train does not move. Could it be the same thing that happened recently to two of our brothers returning from Palermo? An anonymous telephone call had announced that a bomb was planted on the tracks.

29 April

The inhabitants of the district of Bari where we are living are fishermen or stone-masons. A great many are unemployed. Solicitous welcome, even exuberant at times. The heart had all it could ask for. Only a few young people in the parish.

The house we are staying in has been abandoned for some twenty years now. No running water, no electricity, no drainage. Take a step, and everything starts shaking. Long cracks run down the walls from top to bottom. Several panes are broken and have been replaced by cellophane. The staircase that climbs up to the roof has been patched with bits of board. With so much rain it is worm-eaten; it is wise to go up only one at a time.

A house bare of furniture is not without beauty: openings in place of doors, a few benches round the room where we eat, an icon in a corner, mattresses on the floor. The kitchen could not be more welcoming; there are two gas-rings on the floor for cooking meals and warming the room.

30 April

Three times a day we have prayer in the nearby church. The people of the neighbourhood come to join us. At evening prayer we discover a 'living icon', a ninety year old woman. For her we have put a chair at the entrance to the sanctuary. She attempts to sing with us. From time to time she raises her arms and those near her hear her whispering: '*Gesù, misericordia.*'

2 May

Every morning we separate to go to work. Most of us have been taken on as street-sweepers; each teams up with an accredited sweeper. A few of us are responsible for welcoming young people who have come from elsewhere to visit us. At the end of the afternoon, we raise the question among ourselves: what is our primary vocation? In the precariousness of this life in Bari, we are searching.

3 May

Visit from the foreman of the street-sweepers. He likes the fact of our working together: it cuts down their working time without decreasing wages. Emptying dustbins and sweeping alleyways gives us entry into the homes.

5 May

The prayer is becoming more and more popular without losing its meditative character. Afterwards we keep people of the neighbourhood for supper: a hundred or so at a time, even if it that means only a little pasta, a piece of bread and half an apple.

7 May

The bishop expressed a wish that once we would take our common prayer to the cathedral. That Romanesque splendour is in itself a hymn of praise. A child reads the Scripture. Children taking part in the liturgy: that brings us near to the Kingdom of God!

9 May

Departure from Bari. Young people of the neighbourhood assure us that the player will be continued every day. Among those who came to the station with us, whom do we find? Several of the street-sweepers; when the train started, everybody began to sing: *'Ubi caritas et amor, Deus ibi est.'*

13 May

Return to Taizé. Temporary insertion into the most normal conditions of a poor parish has not stopped providing us with food for thought. Isn't it from within that the unique communion called the Church is reawakened? Not knowing how to express this reality in words, we have tried, by going to Bari, to make it concrete by our life.

REAWAKENED FROM WITHIN

Reawakened from within

How often, in the daily dialogues with young people from different countries, does the same question come up: 'Why do you love the Church; its structures hurt us so much?'

Should those who at times suffer from the Church run away from her? But is not running away from the Body of Christ bound to lead to abandoning the Risen Christ on the roadside? Remaining within, with infinite courage, is that not the way to transform rigid structures?

A first-century Christian had grasped that a fundamental reality which, in the end, sets everything in motion, was communion in the Body of Christ. 'The reality is the Body of Christ,' writes Paul to the Colossians, 'and let no one try to deprive you of it.'

Why do we love this communion to such a degree? When it is radiant, it makes visible Christ's own face. It does not exist for believers only, but for all human beings. It is a communion within which kindness and the spirit of mercy are born, and through which are stimulated not only hope rooted in Christ, but also a fine human hope.

Over the past few years, in modern-day societies that are becoming more and more anonymous, many little groups of Christians have sprung up. They are a kind of antidote to a secularized world. With the freshness of the Gospel, these groups bridge a gap between faith and life. Forms of commitment adapted to a rapidly changing world are discovered in them.

A quality of extreme fragility is an inevitable feature of these little communities because of the provisional nature of their life. In order to survive, some of them turn into exclusive little circles with positions which cut them off on all sides. Provided a few feel that they get along well together, they are ready to jump on any band-wagon however esoteric its form. When Christians are fragmented into such tiny particles, what happens to communion in the Body of Christ?

Elsewhere, the large communities called 'parishes' do not exactly engender enthusiasm. On our travels across the continents, one cannot help but notice that the great majority of Christians normally meet for worship in these large local communities. But the young are ill at ease in them when their aspirations are not recognized and they find no scope for their energies. They are bored in the churches, and boredom is spiritual suffering.

Might we not be in a period of new birth and growth regarding common prayer? If the abundance of words in churches is a cause of fatigue, we will soon be obliged to have more and more singing in our prayer.

If young people found they could join in the Eucharist, at least every Sunday, and continue the prayer by staying in church and singing, they would already be creating a space of worship.

PRAYER

What do you ask of us, Lord Christ? Above all to carry one another's burdens, and to entrust them to you in our prayer, which always remains poor.

You welcome all who come to you with their burdens, and it is as if, anytime, anywhere, you welcomed them into your house in Nazareth.

When we let ourselves be welcomed by you, the suffering servant, the inward eye perceives, beyond our own confusion, a reflection of the Christ of glory, the Risen Lord.

And we are brought to life each time you visit us by the Holy Spirit, the Comforter.

JOURNAL: 2 JUNE–25 AUGUST 1978

2 June
Little Françoise, who comes and kneels by me for the common prayer, sometimes utters words that are captivating. This morning she said: 'When you are close to the altar, you feel such a lot of things.' She lives next door; I have known her since she was born.

15 June
Arrived yesterday in Moscow with Thomas and Armin. We couldn't wait to be able to go into the churches. In church, Russian Christians seem to be swept along by a tide of sheer fervour. People continually make the sign of the cross. They come and go to venerate the icons with deep prostrations. This whole style of worship, a far cry from Western efficiency, is like the imploring of a contemplative people.

16 June
In the train from Moscow to Leningrad, a night in a dream world. It is not possible to make the journey by day. But in

these northern latitudes, the night is very light. Through the window I watch a procession of farms, their wells topped by a long arm to raise the water. The isbahs look dilapidated. People begin to work at dawn.

17 June
Touched to discover so many young people in Leningrad Cathedral. Bishop Nicodim asked me to speak. I said to them: 'If Christ were not risen, we would not be here. There would be nothing in the whole country of the burning confidence which is yours.' Just before that, I addressed those who will soon be priests: 'The more you walk with Christ, the more you will be led on to the mountain of temptation. He himself was there. The closer we draw, invisibly, to the agony of Christ, the more we bear in ourselves a reflection of the Risen Lord.'

20 June
Conversation with Armin in the plane returning from Moscow. How ever have you kept this river of communion flowing on in you without interruption for the fifteen years we have been together? His reply: 'When I was very young I used to run the eight hundred metres. After about six hundred metres you generally flag – heart, legs and lungs won't go any farther. To do the last two hundred metres you've got to keep close to the trainer and not allow a space to build up, no gap. In the same way I make sure that there's never any gap between Christ who is ahead of me and myself.'

6 July
Yesterday evening, short shower of rain, the first for weeks. Is it going to interrupt the enchanting Sahara weather? Is the splendour of a Burgundy enveloped in flaming summer about to disappear? The heat of the evenings has faded away. A

breeze is blowing through the lime trees, enclosing them in cool shadow.

8 July

Brought back a new symbol from Moscow. On Friday evenings, lay the icon of the cross on the floor, go and place your forehead on the wood of the cross, entrust to God, by a prayer of the body, one's own burdens and those of others. In this way keep company with the Risen Christ who continues to be in agony for those in tribulation throughout the world.

If the young, once they are back home, would meet every week, faithfully throughout their lives, to pray with others around the cross, they would lead God's people to become a contemplative people.

20 July

In the dormitory, before we slept, conversation on what God can make out of our childhood wounds. When I go every evening from one brother to another to say good night, we sometimes talk like this.

The dormitory is as beautiful as a starry sky: darkness dimly lit by the light of the icon and the little lights of those who like to read.

6 August

We were outdoors, under the trees, just ending the last prayer of the day when Alain came and whispered in my ear: Paul VI is dead. We knelt down again to pray.

Although he was aged, there was within him a mystical passion for the future of humankind. Every time I spoke to him about the young, he was all attention. He understood their searching. No warnings from him. He expressed his confidence in them. In 1969, when we were faced with the idea of proposing a 'council of youth', he repeated twice over:

set it going. He had received reports on us and they were not always favourable; his confidence in us was unshaken.

One day, long before he was pope, we were talking about the difficulties concerning the celibacy of priests in some parts of the world. Then, pointing at the crucifix, he pronounced these words: 'If things are going badly, it is because we who have great responsibilities in the Church crucify him so often.'

One simple incident comes to mind again. During the Vatican Council, he knew that every day we used to receive bishops at table to exchange ideas. One evening someone from the Pope's household arrived with a case of apples and pears which Paul VI wished to share with us and our guests. Though we accept neither gifts nor presents, how could we refuse that?

7 August
For whoever has learned to love, for whoever has learned to suffer, life is imbued with serene beauty.

8 August
Thrilling visit from two young people who, in their own country, know what it is to be interrogated by the police. 'Happy the persecuted . . .' They are a living image of this Gospel saying. If we are afraid, one of them asserted, all is lost; no one will ever rob us of our inner freedom, not interrogations, not imprisonment.

12 August
Funeral of Paul VI. After going to pray in silence before his mortal remains, on leaving St Peter's Basilica with Max, we saw Giuseppe Roncalli, the last of the brothers of John XXIII, going in. We love one another dearly. Together we returned to the body of Paul VI.

As he gets older, Giuseppe Roncalli looks more and more like Pope John XXIII. Seeing these two faces near one another, I imagined, in the eternity of God, the reunion of John XXIII and Paul VI.

18 August
Back at Taizé, the Italian television came to interview me and asked what I expected of the man who would soon be elected the next pope. Before me I have the text or my recorded answer:

'I would like to be present in heaven at the meeting of Pope John XXIII and Pope Paul VI. Those two men complemented each other so well that together they would give something of the picture of the pope we are looking for.

At Taizé we would like the pope to be so much the father of all, so universal, that he does not allow himself to be imprisoned by the strong resistances, either from the old divisions of Christians throughout the world, or from the new ones. Our hope is that he try to be so much the father of all that we can easily recognize in him a reflection of the face of God. By his life may he awaken to God the greatest possible number of people on earth.

How can the pope ensure the life of Christ in the younger generation, the continuity of Christ throughout history? How can he not be too affected by those who, unable to understand a man turned towards the future of humanity, could well try to pull him back by his sleeves and by his cassock saying "stop here, stand still, go no further."

Ensuring the continuities of Christ means living them out in the great living tradition of the Church and thus joining the old as well, those who received a different training in their youth. To follow only the tendencies of the younger generations would be to create segregation, and then the pope would no longer be the father of all. My hope is that the pope will allow a kind of mystical call to live within himself, be a man turned towards the development of humankind while being entirely conscious that he is ensuring the continuities of Christ through a long Church tradition.

If I love the Catholic Church so much, it is first and foremost because she has been throughout her history, even with the most difficult popes of the time of the Reformation, the Borgias, the Church of the Eucharist. She has made the Eucharist into a source of unanimity of the faith down to the present day.'

25 August

Receiving along with my brothers so many young people at Taizé means being for them above all listeners, never spiritual mentors. Anyone who would set himself up as a mentor could well fall into that spiritual pretentiousness which is the very death of the soul.

Yes, refuse to monopolize anyone at all for oneself. The Virgin Mary shows us a gesture of offering: she did not keep her Son for herself, she offered him to the world.

Often we know little of the context in which the life of those who confide in us is unfolding. That is not the important thing. In any case, to answer them with advice or by categorical 'you musts' would lead them astray. Listen to them in order to clear the ground and to prepare in them the ways of Christ.

Today, after listening to young people, Emile and I were walking down from the church to the house. And we were saying to one another: if, when they left, the young would have discovered the gift placed within them . . . if they in turn had the burning desire to make straight for others the ways of Christ . . .

IN EVERYONE, A UNIQUE GIFT

In everyone, a unique gift

Like each and every one of us, Jesus needed to hear a human voice saying: 'You know that I love you.' Three times over he repeated to Peter: 'Do you love me?' Assured of Peter's love, Jesus entrusted him with the Church: 'Feed my sheep.'

To love Christ is to receive from him, immediately, a greater or lesser share in a pastoral gift. God entrusts to everybody one or more other persons.

This pastoral gift, however small, is a source from which to draw the inspirations to communicate Christ. It allows him to accomplish his pilgrimage in the whole human family.

Children themselves, without being aware of it, transmit an image of the living God.

Exercising this pastoral gift means above all listening. Listening to what in the other hurts him about himself. Trying to understand what is beneath the other's heart, until even in earth harrowed by tribulations he can perceive God's hope, or at least human hope.

And it often happens that the one who listens to another is himself led to the essential, and the other never even suspects it.

Growing old. Exercising intuition over a whole

nfetime of listening. And in the end understanding, almost without words, those who come to confide in one.

Listening can bring a mystical vision of the human being, that creature inhabited by both frailty and radiance, fullness and the void.

In each one, a share in a pastoral heart. In each person, unique gifts. Why doubt one's own gifts so much? Why, in comparing oneself with others, desire their gifts and go so far as to bury one's own?

Today a technological age intensifies an acute sense of success and failure. A disposition to get on in the world and to compare oneself with others are inculcated from childhood. Anyone who does not succeed according to society's standards feels condemned and is disappointed that he does not have somebody else's gifts.

Comparisons sterilize. Wishing for another's abilities induces us to become incapable of discovering the gifts in ourselves. Discredit yourself and up come sadness and discouragement.

How is it possible to lose self-esteem, when the Spirit of life is pouring gifts into every one of us? The loss of self-esteem suffocates a human being, shackles his vital energies, and goes as far as to make it impossible to create.

To react against this by overestimating oneself, by seeking social prestige, for instance, is not a way out. Overestimating oneself under social pressure or because of the judgements of those around us, forcing one's gifts artifically, would be like forcing a plant in a hothouse.

There is a way in the Gospel where we meet the gaze of Christ. It has a name: the way of consenting.

Consenting to one's own limitations, of intelligence, faith and ability. Consenting also to one's own talents. That is how strong creations come to birth.

Lord Christ, come, by your Spirit of life, and bring to full flowering the gifts placed in each person.

You take us with our hearts just as they are. Why should we wait for our hearts to be changed before we go to you? It is you who change them. And you offer us all we need to heal the wounds that tear us apart: prayer, hymns, forgiveness and the springtime of reconciliations.

JOURNAL: 31 AUGUST–16 NOVEMBER 1978

31 August
In our vocation, each brother is like a link in an endless chain.
What one cannot manage, another takes up.

5 September
Waiting to be received by John Paul I, we conversed with
Bishop Nicodim of Leningrad. We recalled that, when he
visited Taizé, he consecrated the icon of the Virgin Mary in
our church. He said that he would come to see us soon.
Shortly afterwards, as he was speaking to the Pope, he
collapsed and died suddenly.

10 September
Yesterday evening, discovered in our church a Greek woman,
Orthodox, seventy-five years old. Overwhelmed by the loss
of the only person she had left in this world, her son, she had
come to pray. In the face of this profound solitude, I said to
her: 'Since we are in the habit of receiving our families in the
house on Sundays, come tomorrow and share our community

meal. And, although it's September, we shall celebrate a Christmas.'

Today, we improvised a Christmas dinner for her. The meal was frugal, but gay. In every family, in every community, it is essential on sombre occasions that some gaiety should always arise.

The old woman told us how, when she went to Sweden for her son's funeral, she held a little icon of Christ and she could only keep on repeating: 'Jesus, you are all that I have.'

17 September
Some young Lebanese are here for a few days, racked by anxiety for their country's future, convinced that no solution is possible by force of arms. They refuse the easy way out for themselves, which would be exile. What can we do for this ravaged people?

16 October
Election of John Paul II. Passionately interested in his contemporaries and so pastoral, he will be able to bring a breath of universality to the Church. During his two visits to Taizé and then during the three days in his home at Cracow, I was able to appreciate his gifts. At Christmas on the way back from Africa, I would like to visit him and say: you are so human, so sensitive; we would like to come to Rome with young people to be better able to support your ministry.

17 October
With dawn the sky descended upon the earth. Nature waits suspended in a still mist. In the distance, leaves form lacy designs on a grey background. Close at hand the autumn colours are already showing in the dull light. In the fireplace the glowing embers crackle and bluish flames spurt from the log.

Common prayer   (Taizé)

Marie-Sonaly at ten months

(Taizé)

The shack on the China Sea — (H. Lachmann)

Brother Roger's grandmother with several of her
grandchildren, 1921 (pp. 52, 53)

(Taizé)

'On Friday evenings, lay the icon of the cross on the floor, go and place your forehead on the wood of the cross, entrust to God, by a prayer of the body, one's own burdens and those of others.' (p. 76)   (Taizé)

The shack in the Mathare Valley (H. Lachmann)

(*opposite*) Brother Roger with Pope John-Paul II (Felici)

The children in the Mathare Valley (H. Lachmann)

22 October

When I arrived this afternoon in front of John Paul II, I said to him: 'Praised be Jesus Christ for giving us such a good Pope!' He answered: 'Brother Roger, come and see me often!' After speaking to all the delegations which had come to Rome for the beginning of his ministry, he addressed me again:

'Before separating we are all going to hold hands as a sign that we want reconciliation. We do want reconciliation, don't we, Brother Roger?'

29 October

Once again we are offered a house, this time in the south of Italy. As always we reply that we accept neither gifts nor legacies. Nothing. We even give away our own personal inheritances.

We suggest that this estate should be left to the families who have been working it for a long time.

From the very beginning of our community life, we have wanted to carry on with almost nothing, in any case with the bare minimum.

From the start we felt obliged never to accept gifts, either in money or in kind. The last conversation I had with my father confirmed me in this. How can I forget the day when, suffering from pneumonia, on the eve of his death, he asked to be raised so that he could talk to me sitting up? One last time he insisted: depending on other people's gifts would be loss of freedom. I remember giving him then the same answer: from the first day, when I was alone in Taizé, I lived from the work of my own hands and, with this in mind, I learned among other things to milk cows.

Living one day at a time also means not letting others sense that there are material difficulties when they are there. If the cash-box is empty, adorn the house with special care, arranging everything in simple beauty.

14 November
Two thousand five hundred Vietnamese and Sino-Vietnamese have been packed in for three weeks now in a small cargo-boat, the Hai Hong, in conditions that make survival daily more precarious. What can be done to give them a home? We would be in a position to house several hundred children and their mothers for the winter. But now we are up against obstructing bureaucracies.

15 November
Exactly twenty years ago, the first of my books to be written at Taizé was published: 'Living Today for God'. Now that I am old, I would say instead: living the moment with God.

16 November
When the tempter whispers in our ear his 'what's the use?' and makes us slip and fall to the roadside, there is always a friend to take us by the hand and pull us up. And in our turn, if one day he slips, we will pull him out of the rut.

THE FIRE OF A PASSION FOR GOD

The fire of a passion for God

The quest for God takes on such different aspects in the different stages of life.

At times, when we tend to speak quite freely to God, prayer appears like a vast ocean to plunge into. That ocean is God.

At other times it is only possible to hold oneself in God's presence in silence.

It can happen too that the arid places, the deserts of prayer predominate . . .

When he seeks God, man is dealing with the realities of the Kingdom. They cannot be measured; they have no beginning and no end. Prayer opens up a boundless communion among the myriads who believe. Through prayer, a relationship with God's eternity is created.

Encounter with Christ can be experienced in the flash of a moment, a moment that passes as quickly as it came, and sometimes is only realized after the event: 'Well! He was there, that's who it was!'

Rare indeed are ecstasies or mystical visions. The miracle lies elsewhere: 'We have never seen Christ, but we love him' (1 Peter 1.8).

Astounding, this reality of the Kingdom almost beyond the grasp of the human mind: Christ dwells in us, but also we dwell in him. Through the Holy Spirit, he loves in us, in our heart of hearts. That is the miracle.

It is impossible to force demonstrations of the Holy Spirit. That would be inevitably to move towards autosuggestion, illusory projections of ourselves. But he is never absent; in all humility, quite simply, just let his presence grow in daily faithfulness, one day after another. And the cry of the early Church rises up: 'Do not quench the Spirit' (1 Thess. 5.19).

To anyone anxious about the poor quality of his praying, I would like to say:

Prayer is not a personal feat. When you pray alone, it can happen that clouds come down between God and you. These clouds have names: rebellion, frustration, a feeling of unworthiness or impotence, loss of self-esteem. So many subjective realities can build a great wall between him and you.

If you forget his presence, are you going to waste your time moaning about your forgetfulness? Surrender yourself to confident trust instead. You can find the Risen Christ everywhere – in the street, at work, in church. Whatever your age and your condition, you can tell him everything, like a child, all that imprisons, all that hurts, all that is weighing down upon many others, near and far. He will clear the way. You won't find this dialogue boring.

In order to pray at all times, day and night, and even when hard at work, don't hesitate to repeat over and over again a phrase or a simple chant: 'Jesus, my joy, my hope and my life;' 'In you, Jesus, joy, mercy, simplicity;' ' *Mon âme se repose en paix sur Dieu seul*' ('My soul can find repose in God, in his peace'); '*Bleibet hier und wachet mit mir, wachet und betet*' ('Stay with me, keep watch here with me; watch and pray'); '*Nada te turbe, solo Dios basta*' ('Let nothing disturb you, God alone is enough').

When, in the desert of your heart, there is nothing but the silence of God, question yourself. Is this the beginning of a turning-point to go forward again?

In the Western world, so rational and scientific, a prayer which is not made explicit in words doesn't seem to be one. But isn't desire for God a prayer? He understands your intention, even when you think you can't pray.

And if you were unable to pray at all, it would still be possible for you to entrust yourself to the prayer of someone else, someone who could well be in the evening of life.

In a technological civilization, there is often a break between prayer and work. When struggle and contemplation seem to be in competition, as if we had to choose one to the detriment of the other, this opposition can tear apart the very foundations of the soul.

A life of communion with God is not lived out in dreams hovering between heaven and earth. Far from forgetting others, it is rooted in real-life situations. It takes upon itself the contradictions of the human condition, as well as those of contemporary societies: fascination with the means of power, success at all costs, an atmosphere of doubt which must indeed be reckoned with.

Sometimes, in their understandable desire to go out to meet a secularized world, local Christian communities and groups thought they had to secularize even their worship. But then, the depths of the human being are not touched. Common prayer can never be a monologue in which, although he thinks he is talking to

95

God, each individual is really trying to put his own ideas across to the others. Common prayer presupposes that everyone, including the one who presides, is addressing the living God.

Prayer is a serene force at work in human beings, stirring, harrowing them, never allowing them to fall asleep or to close their eyes to evil, to wars, to all that threatens or attacks the weak of this world.

Anyone who follows in the steps of Christ lives both for other people and for God. He does not seek to separate prayer and action.

PRAYER

Lord Christ, if we had faith enough to move mountains, but no charity ablaze in our hearts, what would we be?
But you love us.
Without your Spirit who dwells in our hearts, what would we be?
But you love us.
By taking everything upon your shoulders, you open for us a way towards the peace of God. And God never wills suffering, nor death, nor human distress. He tells us over and over again: 'My love for you will never disappear.'

JOURNAL: 17 NOVEMBER 1978–1 JANUARY 1979

17 November
When you are too shy to ask for forgivness, why not dare to make a simple little gesture that needs no words: hold out your hand for the other to make in it the sign of forgiveness, the sign of the cross?

19 November
Yesterday, night of prayer in Munich Cathdral before leaving for Africa. A sea of heads everywhere, even in the pulpit, where young people were perched.

When the time comes to address a crowd of people, in order to overcome my shyness I say to myself: stand there like a child, the child you once were when your oldest sister taught you to read and write . . .

At the end of the prayer, the young people did not leave the church, but went on singing meditative chants. We left, my brothers and I, at about one in the morning: a flood of icy cold air was surging through the open doors. But the young people prayed on till dawn.

There are young Germans who feel they are not accepted

by other nationalities. Many Germans have an exceptional ability to get things done. And too, there has always been a vein of mysticism in the German soul. When these two gifts are united to the point of becoming one, the young of this country can be an incomparable catalyst of reconciliation in the world.

23 November

Johannesburg. Visited Soweto. Here poverty consists, much more than in a lack of material things, in the segregation which forces a million blacks to live together in this district.

Meeting with a young black just out of prison. The whites are afraid of us, he said. They try to force us to accept their scale of values. But these values are materialistic and individualistic, they go counter to ours. We blacks want to express the brotherhood of all. And so, in our tradition, people of the same age group are our brothers and our sisters, those younger are our little brothers and sisters and those older are our fathers and mothers.

The whites have brought their conqueror mentality with them, he continued. Among blacks, when a tribe was driven out of one territory, it was only to pasture the flock, never to conquer the land. The land always belonged to everyone. There was never any idea of subjecting one tribe to another. In the last few years, the spirit of fear and mistrust has grown and led to a situation where war and violence have become institutionalized. This situation often produces acts of violence and law suits. There is fear and bitterness. In the end some leave the country.

Confronted with this situation, he concluded, we have discovered the necessity of that moral force, forgiveness. The whites have learned little about how to forgive. To build peace we need leaders of great moral strength and great insight. It is there that we discover the need for the grace of God in our lives.

Before leaving him, I asked him what he expected from us Europeans. His reply: Europeans think the whites have brought everything, technology as well as Christianity. They think the whites made the blacks, not God. You must get to know blacks. It's not easy, because blacks want to show who they are, while whites want blacks to be a copy of themselves.

24 November
Unforeseen visit to the Cape. Only yesterday I learned that we were expected there. In a black neighbourhood where we thought we would be meeting just a few friends, a whole crowd had gathered for prayer. They were singing. Human voices can express the call from the depths more powerfully than anything else.

African priests and pastors of all denominations welcomed us on a platform and handed me the microphone. I alluded to the African man of God my parents met one day when I was five years old. He had blessed me. After that my mother often used to say: in Europe the faith is disappearing, but the Gospel in all its freshness will come back from Africa. I assured them that today that blessing of long ago was finding fulfilment.

Then someone else spoke. But I said to myself: my words were so inadequate. I asked the two brothers who were there, Alois and John, if I should take the microphone once more. They said yes. I tried then to express all that was in my heart by a gesture. I explained to the Africans: I would like to ask your forgiveness, not in the name of the whites, I could not do that, but because you are suffering for the Gospel and you go before us into the Kingdom of God. I would like to pass from one to another of you so that each of you can make the sign of the cross on my palm, the sign of Christ's forgiveness.

This gesture was understood immediately. Everyone made it, even the children. It seemed to take an eternity. Spontaneously they burst into songs of resurrection.

26 November
Nairobi. The shanty town we want to live in is called Mathare

100

Valley. It is the biggest slum in the city. The poorest in all Africa, some say. A hundred thousand people are piled up on the slope of a small valley. People kept on telling us it was a dangerous district, where fear, violence, drunkenness and theft were rife and where it would be impossible to stay. No white had ever lived in Mathare Valley.

Paddling through the mud on our first visit, we were attracted by a shack chained and padlocked. It was in fact available for renting. The owner had found another for himself. He told us that until today, he had been hesitating about leaving this one. 'Now that you are here,' he added, 'I realize that if I have been waiting, it was for God.' And he rented it to us.

The shack looks out on the muddy path where everybody throws their rubbish.

28 November

A few hours in the home of the 'Little Sisters of Jesus' in a Masai village. Their hut is so low that you can't stand up in it. It is made of branches covered with earth and cow dung, and set in the only bit of shade, under a large tree. The village chief made that decision. Around the huts, high brushwood protects the village from lions and panthers. There has been a drought for the last seven years. The cows barely manage to yield two litres of milk a day; the men take them at the crack of dawn to distant pastures. In one of the huts, a woman suffering from chronic anaemia is expecting a baby any minute. She is lying on her back and gazing vacantly into space.

We nearly found the village empty. The tribe is nomadic, and this very morning it was due to move on, but the departure was postponed at the last minute.

The 'Little Sisters' have become nomads with the nomads. Women have less difficulty than men in holding out in such wretched surroundings. Men are so overwhelmed by human distress that sometimes they buckle under. Not knowing where they stand, they throw themselves into a whirl of

101

activity. Women are better able to enter into all situations, and they are also accepted more readily by women and their husbands, which allows them to hold out.

29 November
The very first evening we discovered, to our surprise, that the shack where we had decided to live in Mathare Valley was situated in the red-light district. The prostitutes there are frequently good mothers of families. So often the outcasts of society welcome us with God's own love.

30 November
Our room has become warm and welcoming. The charred planks are covered with cardboard. On the beaten-earth floor we have laid straw. It makes a golden surface. The icon of the Virgin, the cross, the reserved Sacrament, surrounded with straw, create a corner for worship.

We took the advice of an African friend who used to live in the slum and took in two young men from the neighbourhood to live with us. At night they can, if necessary, explain our presence in their own language. They are careful; to answer a knock they don't open the door, rickety though it is.

1 December
The noise is incessant, even at night, worse still on the first days of the month, when the men spend part of their wages in the little drink-shops around us.

2 December
All day long, the children run around outside the shack. Our door is always open. As last year on the China Sea, our life is

there for all to see. Passersby take a look, stop for a moment, speak to us. At the hour for evening prayer, the shack is full and people stand all around outside.

3 December

Leaving her transistor on at full blast in her shack, a woman, one of our near neighbours, often stands outside and takes part in the common prayer. Like other women in the district, she has a child but no husband. Today she asked someone who had come to see us: 'Tell me what there is deep down in those men.' There are saintly women who have God's life in them without knowing it.

4 December

The nights are cold and the beating of the heavy tropical rains on the corrugated iron roof often deprives us of sleep. There are so many leaks we can't cope with them all. With his customary attention to details, Hans is always hurrying around to arrange pots and pans to catch the water.

6 December

Our group is made up of seventeen nationalities. Together we are writing a text for young people, and so we look for ways which would allow us to jump the walls of religious or racial entrenchments. A young African was saying this afternoon: 'Here we are undermined by tribal divisions, and along come more divisions imported from Europe in the name of the faith; in Kenya, there are more than three hundred tiny autonomous churches.'

12 December

Viruses have made their appearance. Several of us are ill. The

103

filth in the middle of the street and the open ditch of dirty water round the shack breed dysentery. The vomiting and high fevers usually begin at night. When I notice the first symptoms, I only need make one leap to the sufferer to attend to his needs, so as not to wake all the others. Caring for your own, a delight.

13 December

This evening, when we had just shut up the shack, someone knocked. One of us went to open the door and found himself face to face with a revolver pointing at him. It happened just when the two boys from the neighbourhood were not there. The woman next door, separated from us only by thin corrugated iron, heard the noise and came out to explain in the local language. It is not the first time that, like the Victory of Samothrace, she strides forward, threatens men and makes them retreat.

25 December

Leaving Mathare Valley yesterday was not all that easy[1]. Fortunately, Denis and Grégoire are going to stay on in the shack and do all they can to persevere for several years.

Christmas Eve in the home for the dying run by Mother Teresa's Sisters in Addis Ababa. They have put down mattresses at the back of the room where sick children lie. Some of the tiniest can't fall asleep. All through the night one of them would turn on the light, another would get out of bed . . . On waking this morning, we could see in their eyes how happy they were to find us there. They realized that three men had been sleeping right next to them. Did they think we were the three Kings?

[1] It was in Mathare Valley that the letter 'The Wonder of a Love' was written. It appears in the preceding volume of this journal and provided its title.

You can read on the faces of the young the gravity of the situation in Ethiopia.

26 December
Before joining the European meeting of young people in Paris, return by way of Rome. Warm welcome from John Paul II in his apartment. God has sent from Poland a man who will be able to open unforeseen ways of reconciliation. With him a life we never dared hope for is being lived.

28 December
To the young people together for the celebrations of the European meeting at Notre Dame in Paris, we pose the question: at the moment Christians are confronted by an alternative; how are they going to answer?

Either, in the image of a humanity exploding into innumerable fragments, the People of God too will remain splintered into multitudes of opposing parts, indifferent to each other, incapable of sharing the joys and the sufferings of the whole human family.

Or else, Christians are going to be reconciled, and widen their solidarity to include all human beings. The Church will become what she is, the seed of a new humanity, reconciled at last.

29 December
As yesterday, evening prayer at Notre Dame. The sacristans are tired after the work over Christmas. Out of consideration for them, we all left together before ten o'clock to continue our celebration at the Church of St Sulpice, where we could stay on longer.

At St Sulpice, for the first time in public, told part of the last conversation with Pope John XXIII. It was in 1963. There were three of us present, Max and Alain were there too. Msgr Dell'Acqua had chosen a day when the Pope was not in pain so that we would have the time for our conversation. We were there to hear from his lips a kind of spiritual testament for our community. 'The Church consists of a series of ever-wider concentric circles', said John XXIII. He did not specify in which of them he saw us. But we understood that in the situation in which we found ourselves, we need not worry, we were part of the Church.

I could not bring myself to tell everything that happened during that last conversation for fear his words would be twisted. Every time situations harden, however, I refer back to them.

When the evening of Pope John's death came, it was as if the earth was opening under our feet. Where in the Church were we going to find such a support?

30 December
Happy as a child to be in the city for a few days. When I was small, we sometimes used to go to my paternal grandmother's in winter. She lived in town. Everything filled me with wonder – the street noises, the comings and goings speeded up by the cold, the tramcar's little bell.

In our country village, on the contrary, signs of life were numbed by winter. In the well insulated stables, the only little window was steamed over all the time. The two or three cows each poor family had were let out only twice a day, to go to the drinking-trough. Every day they sent me out, well muffled up, into the garden which had been put to sleep by the frosts. As soon as the snow began to melt for the first time, I tried to make a guess at the first forerunners of the bursting life of spring . . .

1 January 1979
For Christians, life is all beginnings. They stand at the genesis of situations; they are men or women of dawnings, of

perpetual discoveries. They keep on waiting when there seems nothing to wait for.

The first signs of life on earth go back something like four thousand million years, the origins of mankind to forty thousand years. With her two thousand years of life, the Church has a short history. We are in the childhood of the Church, with all the clumsiness and stammerings of childhood.

A CHILDHOOD OF THE CHURCH

A childhood of the Church

Speaking of the realities of the Kingdom of God, Christ said: only those who receive them with a child's heart can understand.

God makes himself accessible to simple hearts who throw themselves upon his confidence. When adults or old people have a childlike soul, they are capable of recognizing a childhood of the Church.

A childhood of the Church in our day: not wasting time being homesick for the early Church, but awakening in the Church of today the spirit of childhood. First and foremost that means simplicity. Also wholehearted confidence and astonishment, through which skilful manoeuverings and compromises melt away. All administrative relationships are transfigured into steps to communion. The spirit of childhood never manipulates and never uses anybody for its own ends. And the Church, even when sorely tried, will not allow sadness and resignation to keep her captive.

Confidence, not resignation. Not inertia, but a kind of inner letting go: abandoning oneself to the living Christ, to his Holy Spirit.

The heart's confidence can be undermined when we

are misunderstood; it develops to the full in continuous rebirths.

Though childhood certainly has no monopoly of confidence, it does contain a measure of innocence which, if wounded, marks us for life. Every experience leaves its mark as on a slab of soft wax.

For God human beings are sacred, consecrated, by the wounded innocence of childhood. Is this not the source from which a person draws the energies to create and to love? Is it not the same for the communion which is the Church?

Sometimes the adult thinks that a pessimistic outlook is proof of seriousness. That means farewell to wonder. How can we still be in tune then with the realities of the Gospel?

A childlike spirit is clear-eyed candour. Far from being simplistic, it is lucid as well. Different aspects of a situation, positive elements as well as negative ones, are not foreign to it. It has nothing childish about it. It is imbued with maturity. It presupposes boundless courage.

The spirit of childhood will not be stopped by the hardened structures of the Church. It looks for ways of passing through them just as, in early spring, the water of a brook manages to make its way across the frozen earth.

O Christ, when you offer us life as reconciled people in the communion of your Body, your Church, you tear us out of our isolation and give us support in the faith of your whole Church, from the first Christians, the apostles and Mary, down to those of the present day.

We thank you for the reflection of your face, in those children who disclose your mysterious presence to us, exposing us to the realities of the Kingdom – an overflowing heart, simplicity, wonder and jubilation.

JOURNAL: 11 JANUARY–15 FEBRUARY 1979

11 January
Council-meeting of the community. We are quite conscious that our existence is still in its formative stages. We can ask ourselves: have we already begun the common life? Or are we just beginning? Or are we going to begin?

14 January
Haunted by a sight I saw more than a year ago in Bangladesh. In a narrow alley-way, a child was crouched on the ground, carrying a baby on one arm, and trying with the other to lift a second baby. When he held them both, he collapsed. An image of the wounded innocence of childhood. Why is it not possible to take care of such children? More than a year afterwards my heart has not recovered.

15 January
With my brothers, went yesterday for the conclusion of our council-meeting at the sisters' home in the next village. Quite spontaneous dialogue with the sister responsible for the

114

community, Mother Marie-Tarcisius. More than ten years ago, though she was already no longer young, she agreed to leave the mother-house of her community to come and join her sisters who were already helping with the reception on our hill. In her, irreplaceable gifts of listening and intuition. She and her sisters bring us the unique experience gathered by a Catholic community over seven hundred and fifty years. Without their presence, how would we ever have been able to take on a reception of guests that never stop growing in numbers? These women accomplish what we never could have done. Without them we would have had to give up all thought of welcoming large numbers.

16 January
Made a note of these lines by Marie Noël, the poet of Auxerre: 'The noblest spirits, and the most nourishing, are made up of a few great shining qualities and hundreds of unknown little miseries on which their qualities sometimes feed, as wheat is nourished by the rottenness of the soil.'

20 January
Ageing people have the chance of becoming like beautiful ripe fruit, well-rounded and a glowing orange. But that requires a childlike spirit allied to the fullness given by a lifetime of maturation. A young human being is like a fruit still green, sometimes with a tartness that is not without its savour.

27 January
Tomorrow, invited to go to the conference of Latin-American bishops at Puebla. As on the eve of the last departure, little Marie-Sonaly said to me: 'Godfather, not go away!' I promised her: 'Another time, I'll take you with me.'

1 February

I thought I would only stay a few days in Mexico, but such a vast amount is at stake in this meeting of bishops. To leave would be a lack of solidarity with these men who are seeking God's design in their day. For them, the option for the young and the poor are not empty words.

2 February

Looking everywhere for two birds to gladden the hearts of the children of the Mexican family where we are staying. This feast day we remember Mary and Joseph presenting the child Jesus along with two doves, the offering of poor people. Finally we found a man who sold us two birds, well tamed; they walked on our hands.

9 February

In the course of one of their meetings, the bishops asked me to speak. I attempted to express my deepest concerns by these words:

'The more we draw creative energies from prayer, the more able we become to stimulate sharing among human beings.

We would be participating in new separations if we were to accept the formation of a Church of the young, or a Church of a class, or a Church of the poor, or a Church of a race, or a Church of elites, intellectuals or others.

In the history of mankind a sharing of spiritual and material gifts has never been more urgent, for world peace if for nothing else.

It is up to us to take part in the aspiration of so many young people driven to the point of anguish by the search for sharing with the masses of the poor. It is up to us to take our place alongside these young people who, otherwise, confronted with the absence of any concrete response on our part, will either sink into the despair of resignation, or into that other despair of violence or of doctrinaire sharing.

If all of us who have responsibilities in the Church decided to prepare a three to four-year plan, with a view to doing away with all assets not essential to the ministry, our concrete commitment would gain in credibility.

Needless to say, the sharing of goods cannot lead to puritanical austerity. That dehumanizes and puts pressure on others by giving them a bad conscience. Sharing cannot make us forget to arrange everything in the simple beauty of creation . . . and art itself is a gift from God.'

15 February
In the last hours of the conference we all felt that its chief value had been, beyond the confrontations between different points of view, the consciousness of having to proclaim the Gospel in the midst of nations whose population is increasing by leaps and bounds.

TAKING RISKS FOR WORLD PEACE

Taking risks for world peace

In this age when the claims of human rights have come home to our consciences as never before, the law of 'might is right' still rampages over the earth. Humanity is experiencing violence, rumours of war, armed conflicts.

In the Gospel, peace bears the weighty name of reconciliation. This word requires commitment and can take us very far. Being reconciled means beginning a whole new relationship; it is a springtime of our being. What is true between individuals goes for nations too. What a springtime a reconciliation of nations would be, especially between East and West!

A whole young humanity on both hemispheres is eagerly waiting for the frontiers that separate peoples to be brought down, and is not afraid to take risks for world peace. All these young people have certain basic characteristics:

In their search for peace, they refuse to uphold sacred egoisms, whether of a continent, a nation, a race or a generation.

They are aware that, among the prerequisites for world peace, the most urgent is a fair distribution of the goods of the earth among all. The inequitable distribution of wealth, especially when held by Christians, is a wound inflicted upon the whole human community. Many ask: how is it possible that Christians, who often come to share spiritual goods, have in general, in the course of their history, managed so rarely to share their material goods?

Among those seeking after greater justice, there are two different aspirations. They are complementary. Some are more inclined to use all their energies to bring immediate help to the victims of injustice. Others are concerned first and foremost with acting upon the causes, the structures which foster injustice.

Young seekers after peace also know that only equal trust shown to all the peoples of the earth, and not just to a few of them, can lead to the healing of the wounds that tear them apart. And so it is essential never to humiliate the members of a nation whose leaders have committed inhuman acts. Essential also is boundless concern for so many men and women who today, as exiles or immigrants, live on foreign soil. If every home was open to somebody of foreign origin, the racial problem would be partially solved.

In order to share material goods better between North and South, to repair breaches between East and West, sincerity of heart is necessary. Who, whether a political leader or not, could appeal for peace and not achieve it within him- or herself? 'Be upright of heart and steadfast,' wrote Sirach the Sage twenty-two centuries ago.

In the critical situations of our time, many are prepared to anticipate, in their lives, trust between nations. They seek in God the energies to persevere; they commit all their inner and spiritual resources to anticipate peace and reconciliation, not on the surface but in the depths. They know that they are not called to struggle with the weapons of power, but with a heart at peace. They refuse to take up partisan positions.

Peace begins in oneself. But how can we love those who oppress the weak and the poor? And harder still: how can we love our opponent when he professes faith in Christ? God moves us to pray even for those who hate. God is wounded with the innocent.

'Love your enemies, do good to those who hate you, pray for those who malign you.' Making one's own these words of the Gospel requires maturity, and also the experience of having crossed inner deserts of our own.

In that ocean underlying human consciousness there is a longing. Day and night, it receives the answer: peace.

PRAYER

Lord Christ, sometimes we are strangers on this earth, disconcerted by all the violence, the harsh oppositions.
Like a gentle breeze, you breathe upon us the Spirit of peace.
Transfigure the deserts of our doubts and prepare us to be bearers of reconciliation wherever you place us, until a hope of peace arises in our world.

JOURNAL: 20 FEBRUARY–15 APRIL 1979

20 February
In our Burgundian winter the almond tree beside the hermitage has begun to blossom. Its branches ooze sap. They are laden with stamens, white flushed faintly pink.

21 February
The faith of humble, hidden people is a pearl of the Gospel, even if its forms of expression can rarely be understood by the privileged. If the fervour of the humble is rejected out of purism, a vacuum is created which is left unfilled. Nothing remains but scorched earth.

28 February
I have just had a conversation in our church with Christians known as 'integrists'. After them, some so-called 'progressive' Christians introduced themselves.

When I was back in the house again, I immediately made a note: love the 'integrists' and the 'progressives' to the same degree. Above all do not keep them both at arm's length.

That would be a nice safe middle-of-the-road judgement, and then we would be good, self-righteous people, not the poor of the household of God.

In a spontaneous conversation afterwards with Pierre-Yves, we pursued the thought.

We said: nobody's life can have depth without openness, and vice versa. If one is aiming only at depth, well and good, but one will not be tapping all the possibilities of universality present in the human heart. If one is seeking only openness, that is important but, however fundamental it may be, it can light fireworks which, in the long run, become blinding.

No openness without depth. No depth without openness. Will those attracted to openness go and visit those attached especially to depth, and vice versa, to try to understand each other?

The same thing is true between generations. Some young Christians understand, better than they used to, that their elders have been formed, even wounded, by a harsh and strict type of education. And there are many adults, often the oldest of them, whose own trials have made them more sensitive, more permeable to the young.

5 March
When I was about eighteen, I became conscious that to mould one's character it was indispensable to find a few guidelines and keep on referring back to them throughout one's life. A person can only shape himself, the unity of the personality can only be built upon a few basic reference-points to which one constantly returns. These guidelines, which were worked out gradually, formed our original 'rule', our first sources:

'Throughout your day let work and rest be quickened by the Word of God. Keep inner silence in all things and you will remain in Christ. Be filled with the spirit of the Beatitudes: joy, mercy, simplicity.'

10 March

Meeting of young people at Barcelona, improvised at very short notice. One thing is obvious: the reception is so warm, it is here we will hold the next European gathering, between Christmas and New Year.

20 March

Villanueva. Two weeks with the young brothers in a poor parish. Harshness of the climate in the Spanish mountains. Harshness of living conditions for the peasants of this village with whom we work in the mornings. In this little town the population is made up mostly of the elderly. The mountain solitude makes them exiles in their own homeland.

2 April

With age the passion to understand what is going on in the depths of the human heart increases.

In this connection, greatly interested in reading the biography of Coco Chanel. Could it be the absence of love from her father which led this woman, born in poverty, to work slavishly in haute couture, driven by the need to amass a huge fortune and to fabricate the legend of the generosity of an obscure father who had abandoned her when she was quite small?

What happened in the life of an exceptional pianist like Clara Haskil to make her believe herself incapable of playing well, when those who heard her were carried away by her dazzling performances?

8 April

Whoever loves admires. Whoever loves is always finding in the other a reason for admiration. Difficulties of character become acceptable accidents.

13 April

Someone who had not been back here for two years made me aware that the prayer time had almost doubled in length. Borne along by so many young people, a few of us brothers now stay in church to continue the prayer by singing on and on. It seems to go on forever, as if it brought us nearer to a fullness of eternity.

15 April

Easter. In previous years, many young Christians had hoped that a sharing of the goods of the earth would become more common. Today, disillusionment is rife, in the face of observable failure in the various nations. We find ourselves before a kind of void, an ocean with no beacon. We know that all tyrants, all dictatorships, all doctrinaires take advantage of these voids in history.

What can we do to fill up part of this void? There is only one way for a grass-roots sharing to spread throughout the globe, and that is to let ourselves be swept along in the wake of a miracle from God.

Sharing, peace, reconciliation, between East and West, between North and South, meet with so much resistance.

In many countries young people, disinterested, with no desire to carve out careers for themselves, will be able to stand like beacons of the Gospel in the midst of the ocean. Animated by their prayerful waiting, their hearts become as wide as the world. Already they are lights shining in thick darkness.

FOLLOW CHRIST, WITHOUT LOOKING BACK

This text was written while we were sharing the life of a poor district in the South of Chile, late in 1979. Its title then was 'Itinerary for a Pilgrim'.

Follow Christ, without looking back

Without looking back, you want to follow Christ: here and now, in the present moment, turn to God and put your trust in the Gospel. There, you draw from the sources of jubilation.

You think you do not know how to pray. Yet the Risen Christ is there; he loves you before you love him. By 'his Spirit who dwells in our hearts,' he intercedes in you far more than you imagine.

Even without recognizing him, learn to wait for him with or without words, during long silences when nothing seems to be happening. There obsessive discouragements vanish, bursts of creativity arise. Nothing can be built up within you without this adventure – finding him in the intimacy of a personal encounter. No one can do that for you.

When you have trouble understanding what he wants of you, tell him so. In the course of daily activities, at every moment, tell him all, even things you cannot bear.

Do not compare yourself with others and what they can do. Why wear yourself out regretting what is impossible for you? Could you have forgotten God?

131

Turn to him. Whatever happens, have the courage to begin over and over again.

If you were to blame yourself for all that lives within you, your days and nights would not suffice. You have something better to do: in the present moment, celebrate God's forgiveness, despite the resistances to believing yourself forgiven, whether by God or by others.

When trials arise from within, or misunderstandings from without, remember it is in the very same wound where the poison of anxiety festers that the energies for loving are born.

If you seem to be walking in a thick fog, waiting for him, Christ, means giving him the time to put everything in its place . . . A fountain of joyfulness will spring up in the desert of your heart. Not euphoria, not just any kind of joy, but jubilation straight from the wellsprings of eternity.

Without looking back, you want to follow Christ: be prepared, in a life of great simplicity, to struggle with a reconciled heart.

Wherever you happen to be, do not be afraid of the struggle for the oppressed, whether believers or not. The search for justice calls for a life of concrete solidarity with the very poorest . . . words alone can become a drug.

Prepare yourself as well, cost what it may, for that struggle within yourself to remain faithful to Christ until death. This continuity of an entire lifetime will create in you an inner unity which will see you through everything.

Struggling with a reconciled heart means being able to stand firm in the midst of crippling tensions. Far from smothering your energies, this kind of struggle challenges you to summon all your vital forces.

Your intentions may be misrepresented. If you remain unforgiving, if you refuse to be reconciled, what reflection of Christ are you giving? Without a prayer for your opponent, what darkness within you! If you lose the ability to forgive, you have lost everything.

By yourself you cannot do much for others. Together, in community, animated by the breath of Christ's loving, a way forward opens up leading from dryness to a common creation. And when a community is a ferment of reconciliation in that communion which is the Church, then the impossible becomes possible.

You try to be leaven in the dough, you try to love the Church, and so often you come up against internal divisions which tear apart Christ's Body, his Church. The mark of those who seek reconciliation is that, following Christ, they long to fulfil more than to destroy, to understand more than to exhort. At all times they remain within, until the very weaknesses of the Church are transfigured.

When divisions and rivalries bring things to a standstill, nothing is more important than setting out to visit and listen to one another, and to celebrate the paschal mystery together.

When you are afraid of being criticized, in order to protect yourself, spontaneously you may react by taking the initiative and criticizing first. Would you make use of the weapon of a guilty conscience, so contrary to the Gospel, to obtain something from another? Try to understand others with that all-important trust which comes from the heart; the intelligence will catch up later.

Far from lighting short-lived blazes, give your life to the end, and day after day it will turn into a creation with God. The further you advance in a communion

133

with Christ, the more you are led to find concrete steps to take in your daily life.

Without looking back, you want to follow Christ: remember that you cannot walk in Christ's steps and at the same time follow yourself. He is the way, and on this way you will be drawn irresistibly to a simple life, a life of sharing.

The Gospel calls you to leave all things behind. But leaving yourself behind is never destroying yourself; it means choosing God as your first love. Simplifying and sharing does not entail opting for austerity or that self-sufficiency which is a burden on others. Nor does it mean glorifying a harsh and abject poverty.

Simplify in order to live intensely, in the present moment. You will discover a zest for life so closely linked to zest for the living God. Simplify and share as a way of identifying with Christ Jesus, born poor among the poor.

If simplifying your way of life were to awaken a guilty conscience because of all you can never achieve, then stop and take the time to think things over: jubilation, not groaning; everything around you should be festive. Use your imagination in arranging the little you have, to bring gaiety to the monotony of your days.

You need so little to live, so little to welcome others. When you open your home, too many possessions are a hindrance rather than a help to communion between people. Wearing yourself out to ensure an easy life for members of your family risks making them dependent.

Do not worry if you have very little to share – such weak faith, so few belongings. As you share this little, God fills you to overflowing, inexhaustibly.

COLOUR BOOKLET

TAIZÉ – trust, forgiveness, reconciliation

Texts by Brother Roger, Prior of Taizé, selected from his many writings, with full-colour photographs on alternate pages.

With 'impressions of a visit to Taize' included at the end, this colourful booklet will help many to come to know more about the ecumenical community, or become an ideal reminder to those who visit 'the place on the hill'.

165 × 165 mm 32pp   ISBN 0 264 66985 1
                                            paper £1.75

SLIDE and CASSETTE

A set of 36 colour slides with approx. 20 minute tape cassette commentary is now available.

ISBN 0 264 67009 4
(RRP inc. VAT £18.75 postage extra)

Published by MOWBRAY
Saint Thomas House, Becket Street, Oxford England.